Nudges from Grandfather

Honouring Indigenous Spiritual Technologies

Chris Kavelin

Copyright © 2016 Chris Kavelin

www.chriskavelin.com

Cover illustration by Martin Buchan

All rights reserved.

ISBN: 978-0-473-35428-2

Because May asked.

CONTENTS

	Acknowledgments	i
	Foreword	iii
	Introduction	1
	Prologue	19
1	The Night a Lightning Bolt Struck	23
2	Wisdom Man in Action	39
3	William Cooper: Champion of Human Rights for the Jews	51
4	A Twenty Year Prayer (Meeting His Highness)	63
5	Diary of Third Meeting with His Highness	83
6	Smokebush	111
7	Vaughan's Mother	139
8	Journey to Turtle Island	149
9	Nudges from Grandfather	159
10	My Father's Wisdom	169
11	Three Visits from Her	175
12	Conclusion	185
	Epilogue	197
	Preview Chaper Book 2	201

Acknowledgements

I want to personally thank and acknowledge the wonderful contributions of the following people in bringing this, my first book, into being.

His Highness Tupua Tui Atua Tupua Tamasese Ta'isi Tupuola Tufuga Efi; Professor Babuuzibwa Mukasa Luutu; Camilla Chance; Kesiko Awasis: Clifford Cardinal; Aunty Mary Anne Coconut; Uncle Boydie Turner; Thokéya Ináẑiŋ: Kevin Locke; Maualaivao Albert Wendt; Wanbli Tokaheya: Ben Rhodd; Mihkwâw Nimiskiw (Pihesiw) Iskwêw: Lisa Michelle Silvers; Tofua'ipangai: Dr Siosiua F.P. Lafitani; the Loyal Russell Tobin; Christine Watson; Whakataumatatanga Mareikura; Marie Waretini; Pikimai Mareikura; Sailau Suaalii-Sauni; Natasha Hanisi; John Clarke; Abe Schwartz; Michael Pearce; Vaughan Panapa; Alfred Khan; Mark Burch; Emily & Wayne Chibwana; Coral & Ovidio Gomez; Debra & Dennis Lee; Lynette Thomas and numerous unnamed individuals; Grandad, and many souls in the next world who contributed to the development of this work.

Foreword

By Kevin Locke*

Pipe Loading Song

Kholá, léčhel ečhúŋ wo!

Kholá, léčhel ečhúŋ wo!

Kholá, léčhel ečhúŋ wo!

Héčhanuŋ kiŋ, nithúŋkašila

waŋníyaŋg ú kte ló.

Friend, do it in this way.

Friend, do it in this way.

Friend, do it in this way.

When (if) you do that, your Grandfather

will come to see you.

Hóčhoka waŋží ogná ílotake čiŋ,

míksuya opági yo!

Héčhanuŋ kiŋ, táku ehé kiŋ,

iyéčhetu kte ló.

If you sit down inside the sacred circle/altar,

remember me.

When you do that, then the things you say

will come true.

Čhaŋnúŋpa waŋží yuhá ílotake čiŋ,

míksuya opági yo!

Héčhanuŋ kiŋ, táku yačhíŋ kiŋ,

iyéčhetu kte ló.

If you sit down with a pipe,

Remember me.

When you do that, then the things you want

will come true.

Foreword

Kholá, léčhel ečhúŋ wo!

Kholá, léčhel ečhúŋ wo!

Kholá, léčhel ečhúŋ wo!

Héčhanuŋ kiŋ, nithúŋkašila

waŋníyaŋg ú kte ló

Friend, do it in this way.

When (if) you do that, your Grandfather

will come to see you.

Mitákuye Oyás'iŋ

All Are Related.

This is a foundational prayer song, often attributed to the White Buffalo Calf Maiden. In this song the Maiden is adjuring Her followers to walk in Her ways, when she says "léčhel ečhúŋ wo!" – "Do it this way." What She is referring to are the teachings that she brought, the 'Lakhól Wičhóh'aŋ', the harmonious, the balanced ways of life that are embodied in Her teachings and the ceremonies that are connected to Her Dispensation. So She says, "Do it this way." And in the next line "nithúŋkašila waŋníyaŋg ú kte" means "And your grandfather will come to behold you, to bear witness to you", so it is a reciprocity that is referred to.

If one is to conduct themselves according to Her Holy guidance then the one Who sent Her, the Grandfather, will assuredly see and witness and respond. The next line where it says, "Hóčhoka", simply means the place from which one is praying. So it's that holy centre, that centre of the universe which is created. So it says when one sits in that place, one must remember Me, she says "Remember Me". Actually it's referring to when you are filling the pipe, and as you are doing that you have to hold the teachings of the Maiden in your consciousness to remember Her and to remember all that that entails. The next part of the song simply repeats that "when you do it this way". The last part of the song says "táku yačhíŋ kiŋ, iyéčhetu kte" - "That which you ask for will assuredly be granted." So it's the promise that when one conducts themselves according to the Heav-

Foreword

enly teachings, this will result in fulfilment of one's heartfelt wishes.

So this is a prayer that really encapsulates and embodies the Covenant, the relationship between Heaven and Earth, which all the Divine Revelators, and Holy Souls and Spiritual Beings have been commissioned to establish amongst the various distinct kindreds throughout time and throughout the world.

*Kevin Locke (Lakota name: Thokéya Inážiŋ, meaning The First to Arise) is a Lakota Elder (Hunkpapa Band of Lakota Sioux) and Anishinaabe. He is a preeminent player of the Native American flute, a traditional storyteller, cultural ambassador, recording artist and educator. He is most known for his hoop dance, The Hoop of Life.

Introduction

I carry willingly the heritage of my Dead
My children have yet to recognise theirs.
Someday before they leave our house
forever, I'll tell them: "Our Dead
are the splendid robes our souls wear."[1]

---

[1] Wendt, A. (2014), *Whispers and Vanities: Samoan Indigenous Knowledge and Religion,* Huia Publishers, p354

Is there a "next world"? Are loved ones who have died somehow still with us?

Introduction

Every Faith and culture speaks of a spiritual dimension; an invisible realm of beauty and light, a place of ancestors and spiritual beings. It is not some faraway place 'out there'. There is no separation, just a thin veil. We are like infants in the womb, growing and developing our capacities until we are born into that realm. Although the infant may be unaware of the next world and think it is alone: the veil between this world and the next is the caul we wear like a cloak, the placenta connecting us with our mother.

From my childhood and youth I was blessed to have Indigenous friendships and relationships, and for a time lived on the Wind River Indian Reservation in Wyoming. While each Faith has beliefs around the spiritual dimension, many struggle to understand what those teachings mean in practical terms. One of the greatest joys in my life has been to witness Indigenous spiritual technologies as lived forms of honouring intimate relationships with those who have passed on. There are many tools for bridging the physical and spiritual realm that all Indigenous communities around the world are gifted with and like communities of scientists around the world have spent thousands of generations crafting and refining.

Some people understand Western science to be 'objective' and 'universal', however there is growing appreciation in the culture of

Western science that scientific understanding is impacted by the very act of observation. It is relative. One might say, understanding is about relationships.

That moment when we have the flash of insight where all the connections are made and when we deeply *know*, we *feel* it in our body. It could be said that we do not know something *until* we feel it in our body. Until universal truths and principles have become localised in our experience, we cannot really be said to know them. Einstein was able to develop his mathematical model of the theory of relativity because when he was a young man he had a dream or vision of what it felt like to ride a ray of light. He then began to translate that subjective experience into mathematical expressions of the universal. In his own later work, Einstein made explicit the importance of subjective experience as perhaps the most important ground of discovery.

It would be a disservice and indeed false to pretend that the perspective of the observer did not impact the nature of what is being observed. While these understandings have emerged with Einstein's insights, and those of others, Indigenous peoples have known this for many generations. It is why stories of lived experience are a form of teaching these spiritual technologies.

Introduction

Within that ancient form of storytelling is both an honouring of the subjective nature of observation and an intellectual humility that invites the listener to explore their own understanding.

After I wrote the first draft of this book I was asked to explain and clarify some of the spiritual principles in the stories. I hesitated for a long time to respond to this before attempting. I remembered a practice of my Elders. When telling their stories, I've rarely, if ever, seen an Elder stop her or his story to explain what it 'means' to those listening. There is a wisdom to this, as each person will take away from the story what they are ready to understand and that which they are not yet ready to understand will remain waiting for their discovery as they mature. To try to explain it before they are ready could actually prevent them from the natural step of learning it in an integrated way in their own experience later. More importantly perhaps, I paused from attempting to 'explain' because I've noticed that every so often in my life, I have a realisation that a fundamental assumption about reality I had was completely wrong. Over time the frequency of these realisations of my ignorance have increased. Why then should I 'explain' what made the miracles in these stories happen? That would be like deciding that I should crystalize one stage of my ignorance as 'Truth'. So I've made a compromise and sometimes explained my current understanding of the spiritual principles at work. My greatest hope is that this book will invite you to further practise your own independent investigation of spiritual reality. Faith, Belief and Trust are not just 'firm thoughts'. They are Practice.

If you want to understand and experience a growing connection of intimacy with those who have passed on it is vital to develop your own practice and reflection of spiritual principles. Without putting your emerging understanding of spiritual principles into practice it is impossible to appreciate or benefit from Indigenous spiritual technologies.

The Faiths and cultures of your ancestors will be important to reflect on as you develop your practice.

In this book I speak from my own experience and practice as a member of the Bahá'í Faith. Sometimes in these stories I mention my specific religious practices as a Bahá'í, however I do not intend to suggest that these stories happened because I am Bahá'í or that my understanding is absolute. Rather this is like a scientist acknowledging that his experiments were from the paradigm of a quantum physicist rather than a molecular chemist. Like branches of science, each Faith provides a framework of meaning and poten-

Introduction

tial practice. Scientists rarely question that there is a reality just because each scientist investigates a different layer of the observable.

Let me share a little story that simplifies some of my current understandings of how those in the next world work with us. When my son Enoch was about fourteen-years-old, we were walking together around the Sydney Opera House in Australia. As we rounded the back of the Opera House and looked out over the beautiful harbour my son turned to me and asked, "Dad, do we believe in reincarnation?" I paused before answering and found myself saying, "You know how I love you, right?" "Yeah" "Well, when I die I won't stop loving you. And when I die my spiritual vision will increase and one of the things I'll be able to see is a better understanding of your true self. I'll see your spiritual gifts and qualities. I'll also have an ability to see where your gifts match needs in the world. You and I can stay better connected if you are praying for me and doing acts of service in this world for me. If you are doing that then I have a better chance of influencing you with my guidance, in your dreams or creative thoughts. Your heart is the perceptual organ through which you see your way towards your goal. So let's say that in the next world I can see that one of your gifts matches that of a girl on the other side of the world, I'll look at her and think "I love Enoch and I'd like to bring those two together." However I can't directly influence her as I don't have any connection with her. However I can look over and see her grandparents in the next world, so I go over to them and say, "Hey you see my son and you see your granddaughter? You see what I see?" and then they will influence their granddaughter to move in

your direction and I will influence you to move in hers. Then one day you will meet and say, "It feels like we met before, like I've known you in a previous life!" and you will experience coincidences and a sense of magnetic connection. So in that sense it is true, you did meet in a previous life, so to speak, because previous generations on both sides worked to bring you together and you will feel that intergenerational connection. When that happens it will be important for you to talk with each other and explore your sense of purpose and shared values. There may be a need in the world that can be fulfilled by your working together. It's important in such moments not to confuse that magnetic feeling for romantic love… because maybe you are meant to be of service to the world together. There may also be romance, but don't get lost in that and lose focus on the service together." I finished and then Enoch looked amazed and said, "I can't wait for that to happen!" I said, "Well I'm not dead yet, don't rush it!"

Introduction

Although there are many forms of Indigenous spiritual technology and each of you reading this will come to understand various forms, I wanted to suggest a particularly powerful tool useful for your investigative practices.

I sometimes refer to this practice as *prayerful action in service to others*.

Let me give some background to how I learned of this before I explain the steps to the practice.

In 2004, Macquarie University asked me to develop a course in their Global Leadership Program called Spirituality and Social Transformation which I've been teaching now for 11 years. When I started to teach that course, I thought, "How I am going to do this? I'm not some expert in this kind of thing." At the time I was also teaching in the Bachelor of Community Management, a course that was offered to Aboriginal students from around Australia, mostly leaders and mature age students from different Aboriginal communities. I was teaching and tutoring in a few courses there and one of my 'students' was Aunty Mary Anne Coconut who is an Aboriginal Elder from Weipa, a remote community in the far north of Australia. She was about sixty-five-years-old and the senior Elder for the Twal Eagles Council. I felt kind of embarrassed that she was my student because I was learning from her. After the invitation came to teach the Spirituality and Social Transformation course I sat down with her and said, "Aunty Mary Anne, I've been asked to teach this course on Spirituality and Social Transformation, do you have any advice?" She said, "Well, the first thing is to let the students know that if they have any challenge that's facing them, anything that they need done in their lives that they don't feel they can do, that they should go out into nature and find some place that's beautiful. Find some place like a beautiful tree and go sit next to that tree. Then say a prayer to God or to their soul, or to whatever their understanding of the 'Other' or 'Spiritual Reality' is and to ask for help and say, "This is beyond me. I need assistance." Then they should trust that there will be an answer of some kind and that when they feel that answer has arrived they should act on that answer."

Within my own Bahá'í tradition I subsequently found that there is a similar teaching. I'll quote that in its full text rather than try to paraphrase it.

> 1st Step: Pray and meditate about it. Use the prayers of the Manifestations as they have the greatest power.

Introduction

Then remain in the silence of contemplation for a few minutes.

2nd Step: Arrive at a decision and hold this. This decision is usually born during the contemplation. It may seem almost impossible to accomplish but if it seems to be an answer to a prayer or a way of solving the problem, then immediately take the next step.

3rd Step: Have determination to carry the decision through. Many fail here. The decision, budding into determination, is blighted and instead becomes a wish or a vague longing.

When determination is born, immediately take the next step.

4th Step: Have faith and confidence that the power will flow through you, the right way will appear, the door will open, the right thought, the right message, the right principle, or the right book will be given to you. Have confidence and the right thing will come to your need. Then, as you rise from prayer, take at once the 5th step.

5th Step: Act as though it had all been answered.

Then act with tireless, ceaseless energy. And as you act, you, yourself, will become a magnet, which will attract more power to your being, until you become an unobstructed channel for the Divine power to flow through you.

Many pray but do not remain for the last half of the first step. Some who meditate arrive at a decision, but fail to hold it. Few have the determination to carry the decision through, still fewer have the confidence that the right thing will come to their need. But how many remember to act as though it has all been answered? How true are these words 'Greater than the prayer is the spirit in which it is uttered, and greater than the way it is uttered is the spirit in which it is carried out.[2]'

After Aunty Mary Anne Coconut made her suggestion and when I discovered a similar practice in my own Faith, I decided I better put this into practice if I'm going to try to teach it to my students. The stories unfolding in this book are some of my attempts to practise this and other spiritual technologies I began to learn as a consequence.

---

[2] Shoghi Effendi, *Principles of Bahá'í Administration*, p. 91

Introduction

A simple way I like to think about these steps is this. Let's say you have a grandfather who is very wise. When you pray to ask for guidance, it's like walking through your home and going to his room and asking him for help. Now if you are caught up in your life and rushing around, you might think of prayer as something you don't have much time for and you only do the first step. That's like rushing to the door of your grandfather's room and saying, "Grandad help! What should I do?!" and then running away before even pausing to hear his answer. So it's important to slow down and not only ask, but pause to listen and trust that he will give you a good answer. Then when he speaks you listen with attention.

Now if you finish the process there and walk away and say "Thanks Grandad! Great answer!" and you don't actually put into practice what he suggested, well you missed the whole point again. You have to put into practice the advice he gave. That's the next step. After that you might make mistakes in putting his advice into practice, and that's ok. You learn from those mistakes and you visit Grandad again and ask for further guidance and clarity on his advice to help you get it right. So you can see it's not just 'practise steps 1-5 and you're done.' You can revisit steps to get clarity and it's actually important to reflect on the results of your actions before returning to ask for further guidance "What's next?" and then taking further steps as you learn. Grandfather will always be there to help, but you have to ask, listen, trust, act and stick with it, reflect and then return to repeat.

Regarding the spirit of the practice itself, along with humility, gratitude seems to be one of the most essential spiritual qualities to develop and express in every step. Gratitude is the opposite of resentment or entitlement. We can start small and even if we don't feel it at first, we can find things to say "thank you" for. That act itself will eventually change the inner thoughts and the feeling will follow. That inner energy of gratitude begins to permeate our thoughts and we then begin to see that the 'broken glass' we were avoiding on our path with fear, is actually diamonds given to us to fulfil our purpose.

A quote on the spiritual quality of purity that I recently reread, reminded me of a sacred wisdom that I learned from my beloved daughter May when she was around four-years-old. When my children were younger I had a practice of spending one-on-one time with each of them and taking them in turns to conferences I go to. I find that giving each child one-on-one time makes it easier to honour their dignity and to answer their questions from a space of respect and discernment. Honouring that they are *spiritual beings in a physical form* creates a powerful self-identity for them. I felt my job as a parent was to help them develop the ability to navigate the world as spiritual beings. When I try to spiritually companion them, they themselves begin to speak from the level of their higher self much more easily. I learned this from my mother, but even more powerfully from my own children.

One of the first conferences I took May to was about eighteen years ago. This was a conference on Eco-Justice (justice for the earth) in Adelaide, Australia. In the first lecture, which was on causes of global warming, I looked over at her and she was sitting in her chair swinging her legs and I wondered how long we would make it through the lecture. I partly worried she must be terribly bored. At one point I felt her tugging on my shirt. We leaned towards each other and she whispered, "What's methane?" I said something about it being a gas, like cow farts, that can trap heat in the blanket of the earth if too much of it escapes into the air. She nodded in agreement with that hypothesis and continued monitoring the accuracy of the lecturer. That moment taught me not to underestimate our children. However, I was in for a much more humbling and awe inspiring lesson from her the next day.

The next day we were driving back home and again she was quiet and leaning her forehead against the window looking at the landscape. I thought maybe she was looking for kangaroos that we had seen on the way down. Suddenly she yelled out, "Stop the car!" "Why?!" I asked with concern. "Someone put garbage on the earth! We have to clean it up!" I felt the justice and compassion in her voice and I had no choice but to be obedient to nourishing those virtues and I pulled the car over to the side of the road. We walked back down the road and she showed me the scraps of McDonald's paper someone had thrown out of their window. We bent down together and picked up the rubbish and put it into our rubbish bag and went back to the car, and I invited her to talk about this new sensitivity for caring for the earth she had discovered. I remember feeling humbled by her fresh discovery of love and sadness for the earth. At one point she again said, "Stop the car!" but added a "More rubbish! Damn those people!" I stopped the car and asked her not to use bad language. She paused, tilted her head and said, "What is bad language?" Oh boy! I thought, How do I explain that?!

As we walked to get the rubbish an idea came to me. Several weeks before, I had mentioned the importance of meditation and learning to listen to our own conscience that guides us. She had trouble understanding what a 'conscience' was. I found myself saying, "You have a little May in your heart who is very wise and knows what is good. If you ever want to know if something is right or wrong, you can ask her and if you are quiet enough and listen she will answer you." She thought a few moments, "I can't hear her!" I told her she will learn to hear if she practises regularly. Some days after this, she announced with victory that she could now ask and hear little May in her heart.

So now during our ride, answering her new question, "what is bad language" I reminded, "remember the little May in your heart?" "Yes." "Well, when you say an angry word it's like a little shadow-cloud comes out of your mouth and it might hover between you and your own heart and then it makes it harder to see and hear the little May in your heart."

She sat quietly for some time as we drove. I remember the strong thoughts in my own mind, Did that make sense to her? Was that accurate guidance? After several minutes she spoke with a clear knowing excited voice that again humbled me. "There are THREE kinds of shadows!" Me: "Huh?", she continued with the energy of childlike wonder, "There are THREE kinds of shadow! The first kind of shadow is the shadow that comes from THINKING a bad thought. The next kind of shadow comes from SAYING a bad thing. But the worst kind of shadow comes from DOING a bad thing!" I was stunned at her wisdom and sat holding that discovery. Then she continued, "BUT! There are THREE KINDS OF LIGHT THAT GET RID OF THE SHADOW! There is the first kind of light that comes from thinking a good thought, the next kind of light comes from saying a good thought and the best kind of light that gets rid of all the shadows is DOING A GOOD THING!"

Sitting here eighteen years later with a grateful lump in my throat and tears blurring my vision, I'm marvelling still, at her young wisdom, which clearly reflected teachings of Zoroaster. I also realise for the first time, that her discovery was possible because she had listened to the little May in her heart and had ACTED in cleaning up the rubbish. Her DOING A GOOD THING enabled her wisdom that day. She taught me that true philosophy must include good action and not just thoughts or words. Purity.

> *For any human being, the purification of character is done thus ... with good thoughts, good words, good deeds.*
>
> \- Zoroaster

Prologue

In the summer of 1987 I had just turned nineteen. I was serving as a volunteer at the Bahá'í World Centre in Haifa, Israel. An Elder African-American leader in the Bahá'í Faith, Magdalene Carney, had invited me to her home for dinner. I looked up to her as an Elder of great faith and humility who had served greatly in education and was a champion of the Civil Rights era. I remember Magdalene's dignity and grace, her nobility and humility, her sense of having seen suffering but of having a great capacity for joy and humour, her abiding determination and unwavering certitude and obedience to God. I also remember her gentleness and genuine kindness that inspired a feeling of safety. If I were a stray cat I would have gone to her house.

I remember that evening I felt I could be open with her to explore my heart's concerns and hopes as an emerging adult, trying to take responsibility for who I was to become in the world. That included talking about dreamtime experiences that seemed significant. One of my concerns was a fear of *ego* getting in the way of pure service.

I was anxious and stuck. It mattered so much to me. Trying to work it all out, at one point I said, "I know that the ancestors and angels of the spiritual realm are all lined up and waiting for volunteers to serve. I know it has very little to do with my actual capacity to serve, but with theirs. They are waiting. I don't even have to raise my arm to volunteer. I only need to wiggle my little finger to say "yes" and they will rush forward. I know a little about what they are capable of. I also know that many great things are likely to be achieved by them even if all I do is raise my little finger; others in this world are likely to think I am doing those great deeds and begin to falsely attribute praise to me. I'm worried that as that praise begins I'll start to believe them and think it's me, and that my growing ego will then actually cut off my ability to serve. I see in you humble service combined with great deeds. How do you get rid of ego? How do you not let it get in the way of doing service?"

Magdalene paused and then said in her soft southern accent, "I just DO IT." Another pause. "Ego will always be there. I say, 'Oh hello, ego. There you are. Aren't you cute?' And then I just do it anyway."

Her simple grandmother's wisdom has endured with me to this day. We all have ego. We will never be rid of it and there is no point in waiting till it's 'gone', or diminished enough before we wholeheartedly throw ourselves into the arena of service. Like Magdalene the champion.

I see her smile a lot.

The stories in this book are about what happened after I finally chose to raise my little finger.

Magdalene might have been smiling from heaven eighteen years later when a lightning bolt struck next to me.

Chapter 1

The Night a Lightning Bolt Struck

On one night in February 2005 at about 3am, I was awake saying my Bahá'í long obligatory prayer. At the point of the prayer, "the letters B and E have been joined and knit together," I had several thoughts and images overlap in the one moment. I was facing an excruciating challenge of feeling love for another person. Our pure friendship and discourses had been such a relief, like breathing spiritual air after having no oxygen for a long time. But I was preoccupied and mixing up what fulfillment in spiritual love would be, with expectations of another person. My anguish had felt overwhelming for some time. I wanted to somehow be liberated from that. I realised that I needed to become detached, to actually change how my mind and heart perceived. In this point of the prayer it occurred to me that I could transform my misplaced attachment by trying to shift my focus to service to *humanity*. Then I had the sudden awareness that I didn't actually love service to humanity in the depth that I should. Thankfully, along with that painful awareness came the understanding that with help and effort, I could actually transform this, this thing that felt like a very deep spiritual human love for one person, *into* a greater love for humanity. I could somehow transform my understanding of reality. Then came a rush of longing, pleading – My heart flared in that moment of prayer, as I felt my own powerlessness to transform.

In that moment a lightning bolt exploded in the back yard, together with a tremendous clap of thunder that reverberated through the house and my very bones. The children startled awake: first May woke up, then Martha and Enoch. I had to stop my prayers to comfort them.

The next day my then brother-in-law came over for a visit and as we drank tea he changed course in the conversation and said, "I've just remembered the time when beloved Dr Ugo Giachery was flying out of Sydney on his way to Samoa. A friend called me late at night and suggested that I come to the airport to see him off, as nobody else knew that he was visiting and it would be a chance to spend some brief moments with him alone. He was an amazing man. Now why did I just remember that?"

I felt those words were meant for me. As he spoke I remembered that in 1988 I had read the book *Shoghi Effendi: Recollections* by Dr Giachery and I wrote a letter to him to express my admiration for his love and devotion in having risked his life in arranging one-of-a-kind building materials to be brought out of Italy during World War II. These materials were used for the superstructure of a Bahá'í Shrine and the International Archives building in Haifa, Israel.

I had ended my letter to Dr Giachery by asking him to feel no need to write me back because I knew he was very ill. Some weeks later a letter arrived from him, penned in his own hand, slanted across the page as he wrote it from his hospital bed. He had written profoundly loving words. His words were so loving and generous that I felt as if I was one of his own grandchildren. He passed away shortly after sending me that letter. I would often recall his words and loving connection and hope that I might do things in this world, that would bring joy to his heart in the next world, even though I felt it beyond my capacity to do this.

I remembered Dr Giachery's letter and felt a coincidence of my brother-in-law's memory occurring the day after the lightning bolt responded to my night time communion. I excused myself and went to pray to ask for guidance as to deeper meanings. *There are infinite ways to ask for guidance, the main point being that whatever way we ask, we create a space for slowing down in our lives and 'listening' with trust. Those in the next world are then able to interact with us. The point isn't so much the form, but the focus, intent and humility of asking. So whether your preference for seeking 'response' to prayer is through nature, or music or listening to children, these are all potential means of interaction with the spiritual realm when done in a good spirit.*

For me in that moment of seeking clarification about the lightning, I felt inspired towards a practice I sometimes use, which is to randomly select a book from my bookshelf of religious writings and open to an unplanned page, and without looking, put my finger on a line then read what it says. What I read doesn't always have obvious significance, but often there is very clear meaning. On this occasion there was clarity.

I got up and went to one of my bookcases and closed my eyes and reached out and pulled the first book that came to my hand. Without looking at the cover I opened the book and put my finger on the lower right hand page and read to see what was there for me. The words leapt out at me: "He then went to an international conference on behalf of the Universal House of Justice. From there he went on to Samoa." It was actually referring to Dr Giachery who eventually formed a good friendship with the King of Samoa, Malieatoa, and was a servant to him and the people of Samoa. My eyes widened in awe. In two weeks I was due to go to an international conference in Canberra. I had been asked to consider presenting a paper there at the UNESCO sponsored conference *Transformations* on the theme of culture and development. I had no idea what the reference to Samoa was about. I then took the liberty to look at the book cover and saw it was *Guiding Lights*, a book with chapters on the lives of various Hands of the Cause in the Bahá'í Faith. I looked at the chapter title I had opened to and saw it was none other than the chapter on the life of Dr Ugo Giachery. My sense of wonder and awe intensified and tears filled my eyes. What was this about?

I meditated and I had the strong feeling there was something important about the upcoming conference that I didn't yet comprehend, more than just an academic exercise. Perhaps I was meant to serve someone there somehow? So I looked at the conference program of *Transformations*, on the theme of cultural diversity and development; two of the keynotes stood out for me, neither of whom I had heard of before. When I saw the profile of keynotes

Professor Anwar Galla and Lillian Holt I felt that I wanted to strive to be of service to them somehow. I wasn't sure of the reason for this, but decided to put energy into action to see what might result. I looked more closely at the profiles of these two people I felt called to be of service to. Professor Galla was a development expert from India (I later heard from him that as a child he was a pick-pocket in the streets and one day he tried to pick pocket someone and they reached out their hand and grabbed his wrist… He looked up and it was Mother Teresa. She then took him off the streets and raised him. Now THAT's how you get into development work.)

Lillian Holt was the first Aboriginal woman in Australia to get a Masters' degree in education and was doing her PhD on Aboriginal humour and was the Vice-Chancellorial Fellow at the University of Melbourne. Not knowing these two people, I prayed and asked that I might be guided in writing the paper I was to present. I prayed as I wrote that it might somehow match needs they might have, hoping that I might be guided to write something that might resonate with their souls. My paper was titled "An Individual Bahá'í Perspective on Spiritual Aspects of Cultural Diversity and Sustainable Development: Towards a Second Enlightenment."

When I arrived at the conference I listened to the keynote presentations and felt further confirmed that these were two very special people and my hope to be of service to them intensified. My paper was being presented at one of four parallel sessions and I prayed that Professor Galla and Ms Holt might be present to hear it. When the time of the session arrived, I scanned the small audience and saw that neither one there. Also, my PowerPoint didn't work so I had to present it verbally. I did my best but felt somewhat disheartened that my hope and energy seemed misplaced. I became humbled in my idealistic hopes.

After my presentation a few people came down to express gratitude for what they heard and to discuss it further. One person introduced himself as Mali Voi, the Sub-Regional Director of Culture for UNESCO based in Apia, Samoa. My heart flared, "So this is what the apparent guidance was for? This was the reference to Samoa? Was I meant to serve this person?!" I went home and, meditating on the encounter with Mali, rewrote my paper six times before emailing him the final draft. Mali wrote back soon afterwards, "Hats off to you! I have read your paper three times …," and indicated that it was of value to him. I felt satisfied that perhaps this work may have assisted him in his path of service of honouring cultural diversity in policy development. I was content and grateful. Little did I appreciate what was to happen next!

Several weeks later I was in my temporary office. The head of the law school at Macquarie University had generously lent me his office while he was on sabbatical so I would have space to write my PhD. The phone rang and I answered it, expecting the call to be for the Dean. It was his office and I had never received calls there. The woman on the phone introduced herself as Christine Watson and said she had attended my presentation in Canberra. Christine was organising a conference and associated art exhibition to be held in one month called, Land: Our Life. "I really enjoyed the way you were able to communicate some of the Indigenous wisdoms so clearly and I would love to have you speak about those things again, but don't have the focus on the Bahá'í Faith this time." I gladly accepted. (By the time of the conference we had been communicating regularly. Christine said I could talk about whatever I was inspired to.)

I returned to Canberra, this time at the Australian Centre for Christianity and Culture and met up with a dear friend, Paul Stevenson, son of the Bahá'í International Teaching Centre member, Joy Stevenson. Paul encouraged me to practise being empty before my presentation and to rely on the guidance of those in the next world to guide my speech in connecting with the hearts of the audience. He also related his suggestion to the methods of Mirza Abul Fazl, a prominent Bahá'í Scholar from the last century. *This method is about being 'empty' – to set aside self so the inspiration of the spirit*

& ancestors can work and be present and synthesized with & by your consciousness.

I felt fear in my stomach as I contemplated what it meant to be empty before my talk, equating it with being 'blank' and speechless on stage. I said prayers for assistance in the midst of that fear and decided to practise courage as I tried to do this.

I reviewed the conference program just as the sessions were about to begin and could hardly believe my eyes. I hadn't told Christine about my previous insight and hope to be of service to Professor Galla and Lillian Holt. As I walked up to the stage for the first keynote panel, I felt even more in awe. I sat down in the only empty chair of three on the podium. To my left was Professor Galla and to my right sat Lillian Holt!! My heart flared in gratitude. I looked at Professor Galla and couldn't sense any way that I could be of service to him that afternoon. I looked at Lillian and felt a sense that she was suffering somehow and that I should focus on her when I spoke.

When I spoke I acknowledged the ancestors with us in the spiritual realm and spoke about how they are exchanging spiritual gifts and healing old wounds. After I spoke, Lillian stood to speak. She related that over the past ten years she had been losing hope because of the political situation in Australia that wasn't lifting Aboriginal people up, but making it harder for them. She later told me that after I spoke she felt a renewed sense of hope. I felt so much joy and contentment in that moment. Perhaps her renewed sense of hope would open doors for her that might help her carry out more things of benefit to Aboriginal Australia. Little did I appreciate what was to happen next!

A week or two later Lillian wrote to me briefly and said, "Chris, I really loved the quote you included at the beginning of your talk. Would you tell me who said that?" I remembered it well as I had memorised it and it formed the opening statement of my Masters Thesis: *An examination of the environmental crisis from a Bahá'í perspective: The balance of the instrumental and intrinsic value of nature.* The quote was from the eminent scientist Ervin László, a leader in Systems Theory, a member of the Club of Rome and co-author of the first book to predict the systemic aspects of the environmental crisis, *The Limits to Growth* (1972). That book was a collaboration between scientists of the Club of Rome who wrote a program they used for one of the first super computers at the Massachusetts Institute of Technology, which predicted that contemporary levels of industrial output would create a future major environmental crisis and economic instability. Twenty years later Professor László wrote *The Inner Limits to Growth* saying that the outer symptoms of environmental crisis were really reflections of an internal human crisis. The quote that resonated with Lillian that I spoke was:

> *Living on the threshold of a new age, we squabble among ourselves for bygone privileges, we seek to satisfy obsolete values in innovative ways. We manage individual crisis, while heading towards collective catastrophe. We seek to change everything on this earth but ourselves.*

I wrote back to Lillian letting her know that it was Professor László's quote. After I sent her the email, a thought occurred to me. If Lillian's mind resonated so much with Professor László's quote, perhaps their minds together might unfold something of great value for the earth. I prayed about it and felt confirmed. But how was I to put Lillian in touch with Dr László? I didn't know him. I had read his book in the late 1990's and he was old then. Was he even still alive? So I decided to Google 'Ervin László 2005' to see what would come up.

The first hit was an NGO website that specialised in advertising inspirational speakers similar to the current TED talks. It had a picture of Ervin László and described a talk he was giving in Paris shortly. Then my eyes widened. Underneath the advertisement for his talk was a caption: 'If you like Ervin László see Lillian Holt in New York' along with a short summary of her topic. My heart raced and I thought, "Ok. I get it. Bring them together." The nudge was heightened by the fact that it was a dynamic web page; when you clicked to refresh the page, a different 'you may be interested in' speaker popped up. But the first time I saw that feature it was Lillian. I prayed again and sought a way to follow through.

I researched Professor László further and found that he had subsequently founded The Club of Budapest, another group of eminent thinkers and Nobel prizewinners. This Club releases statements to influence enlightened environmental policy and gives awards to small grass roots environmental initiatives around the world. As I read the website further looking for Professor László's contact details, I saw a link to an associated institution also founded by Professor László, the World Wisdom Council. I clicked on that and looked at the members, seeing many Nobel Prize winners. Mikael Gorbachev was the Chair. There was a contact detail for Dr László's secretary, Wolfgang, so I wrote to him asking him to pass on my message to Professor László. In my email I wrote that I noticed that there were no Aboriginal people on the World Wisdom Council and suggested that he may wish to consider appointing Lillian Holt.

Several months passed and I thought my message had vanished into cyberspace. Then one night I was checking my email during a break at my night job as a security guard at Bond's underwear factory, and there was a message from Professor László! I laugh remembering the contrast between my mundane location and my soaring spirits. Professor László wrote back asking if I would consider being the Club of Budapest representative for Australasia (I have to admit I never followed that invitation up.) He thought it was a wonderful idea to appoint Lillian Holt to the World Wisdom Council and told me to consider it done. He asked me to put her in touch with him and said that there was a World Wisdom Council meeting in December (2005) in Switzerland. I contacted Lillian to give her the good news and to introduce them properly so they could begin to make the arrangements. Lillian kindly invited me to come with her to participate in the World Wisdom Council meeting. (Imagine that!) Unfortunately, because of needs operating in my family at that time, I couldn't go.

Lillian flew to Switzerland. During their meeting I prayed as I made my rounds patrolling the underwear factory. I felt tremendous joy and gratitude to all the angels like Dr Giachery and Shoghi Effendi who, I felt, had made these things happen. I'm sure that neighbours may have wondered at the laughter echoing around the factory that night. If they listened carefully they would have heard more than one voice laughing.

I had always meant to thank Christine Watson, who organised the

Land Our Life conference and exhibition that put me on the same stage with Lillian. Christine is devoted to healing the Australian land and people and to honouring spiritual connections between humans and land. The *Land Our Life* art exhibition and conference she organised had participants surrounded by artwork on the same theme, enabling them to consider intellectual, emotional and spiritual aspects of their relationships to land; this affected many people profoundly. I never had the chance to thank her and describe the extent of what happened for me afterwards. I lost touch with her. So as I began to feel called to write this story down I realised I needed to find her and thank her; to let her know how her act of service had given rise to these positive developments in the world.

Though I tried to find her contact details I didn't have any luck and my emails to people that might know her weren't answered. Finally while writing this chapter in 2015 I spoke with a young man on the phone at the Centre for Christianity and Culture where *Land Our Life* had been held, and when I told him I needed to get hold of Christine Watson he said, "Oh! My mother is having lunch with her right now! I'll text her and get her to call you." So when I arranged to fly to Canberra in February 2015, just shy of 10 years after we last met, we agreed to meet at the Aboriginal Tent Embassy, which is in front of Old Parliament House. My taxi dropped me off and I saw Christine get out of her car. Before we could walk the ten meters to hug, dozens of Aboriginal people walked out of tents and then between us as they were beginning a march to Parliament to protest the new Stolen Generation of Aboriginal children. Painted faces and Aboriginal flags waving fluttered across my vision as I looked across at Christine. It was very surreal.

Christine and I hugged and we had coffee. As we were sitting down and before I had a chance to tell her the story, Christine asked: "How did we meet again?" I reminded her that we met originally at the Transformations conference ten years ago to this month. She looked surprised and raised the bag strap she had over her shoulder and held out the bag she was using. It was the conference bag from *Transformations* ten years ago. All this time she kept it because doing transformational work is so important to her. And maybe she was holding on to it until I could tell her the story. As she held out the bag I said, "I've got a story to share with you about that."

Chapter 2

Wisdom Man In Action[1]

In 2005 I was walking down the hallway of Warawara, the Department of Indigenous Studies, at Macquarie University, Sydney, Australia. I was on my way to see Sam Altman in his office. Sam was the coordinator for the Bachelor of Community Management. As I approached his office I was reading a paper in my hands. I looked up as I neared his office and realised Anita Heiss, the Indigenous Author-in-Residence, was standing in his doorway talking with

---

[1] Camilla Chance, author of *Wisdom Man: Banjo Clarke as told to Camilla Chance*, asked me to write this true account as a chapter for another book in production *Wisdom Man in Action* which follows on from her first book on Banjo Clarke (see http://www.wisdommanbook.com/)

him. She seemed to be speaking with a deep sincerity, and I wasn't sure if it was a personal moment; yet I was in the awkward position of having just looked up as I arrived. I briefly paused to decide how I could respect their space (do I keep walking?), she turned to me and kept talking as if I was now part of the conversation and so, well there I was. She was saying, "and I'm on the plane reading and connecting to the incredible life of Banjo and his Faith…" When Anita said, "Banjo" I felt wonder and I remembered that three years earlier I had been asked by Terry Widders, a good friend and a supervisor of my PhD thesis, to share my understanding of my 'cultural blindness' with his class of mostly American students (about 90 of the 100 students.) In preparing for that I had come across a website that showed the face of Elder Banjo Clarke and his face mesmerised me. There was something special about this man. I had included in that presentation, a picture of his face and his words:

> *Without the land we'd be lost people. It's a spiritual thing. That's where you're born, that's very sacred. That's your spiritual home 'til the day you die.*

I had wanted the students to appreciate the difference between being tourists and having reverence for the land they were on. Banjo's love for the land shone in both his face and his words.

So there I was three years later with Anita talking about the amazing way he lived his life; his certitude, his faith. She told me Banjo was a man of great compassion and forgiveness. She explained that she had just returned from Melbourne Australia, where she had helped give out the Unsung Indigenous Hero Award to a woman named Camilla Chance. The Award is given to Aboriginal people who have selflessly done something of service for others. This was the first time that this award was given to a non-Aboriginal person. The reason was because Camilla had sat with Banjo for many years; at his request she put his words into writing, into a book called *Wisdom Man*. *Wisdom Man* became a best seller, and Camilla had arranged for all the profits to go to Banjo's family and towards a centre that would teach people about the forest that he loved.

In that hallway, Anita suggested I read the book, which I did. I was fascinated by Banjo's noble history. He was descended from Queen Truganini of Tasmania. He told the stories of her escaping the genocide of her people, going to Melbourne and then to Warnambool. Banjo told stories of the generations since then, his experience of being raised in the bush, experiences of racism, constant need to forgive people who wronged him personally and for their actions in general. While I was reading the story of his family and the generations, I remembered a TV series that I saw as a child in the U.S., called *Roots,* which followed the life of an African family from the time of their freedom as noble people, to enslavement, emancipation and fight for equality. *Roots* had given me a deeper sense of story of connection and empathy. As I read *Wisdom Man* I thought to myself, "This book would make a wonderful film that could help Australians to feel that sense of connection and love as well."

The next day I went over to Anita's office with excitement and told her what had occurred to me; then I said, "I'd love to help them make it into a movie, maybe I could do something to help? I don't know anything about how movies are made, but maybe I could do some fund raising or just make coffees or .. whatever I could do to help." Anita smiled and said, "I'm sure that the movie rights for the book already belong to Penguin and ." My face may have looked a bit sad, and then she said, "But I can give you the contact details for Camilla and you can speak to her yourself." So I wrote to Camilla letting her know the effect *Wisdom Man* had had on me and what I hoped. She wrote back within minutes! She said, "Call me now…" and gave me her mobile number.

I called her and she said, "We have been waiting for the right person to come along. Banjo says you are the one we have been waiting for and you will help us make this into a movie." I was stunned, first of all, Banjo passed away in 2000, and this is 2005, so how could he have said that I would help make it into a movie? I said to her, "What? Me make it into a movie? I don't know anything about making movies though... *I just wanted to help*... what would I do?" She then said, "Before Banjo died he said he wanted Phil Noyce to be the director of the film." I asked her who Phil Noyce was and she said he directed the movie *Rabbit Proof Fence*.[2] "You could start by sharing the book with Phil and asking him to direct the movie." "Where do I find Phil?" She told me he had an office in Fox Studios in Sydney, which was actually pretty close to where I lived. I agreed I would do my best to get *Wisdom Man* to him.

After our call I sat down and said some prayers and meditated. How did this happen? How could I possibly accomplish this? While I was sitting silently in contemplation after the prayers I remembered that the next day was my birthday. I also remembered that in the previous year something extraordinary had happened on my birthday when I said some prayers and offered myself up in service to help some people. I remembered Shoghi Effendi's five steps to prayer, *which included trusting we would be guided and acting with complete faith on whatever inspiration came after prayer.* I finished the night by saying some prayers for Banjo, and recalling `Abdu'l-Bahá's words. About people who have passed to the spiritual realm, He says:

> *Those who have ascended have different attributes from those who are still on earth, yet there is no real*

---

[2] Rumbalara Films, 2002

separation. In prayer there is a mingling of station, a mingling of condition. Pray for them as they pray for you! When you do not know it, and are in a receptive attitude, they are able to make suggestions to you …[3]

I went to sleep hoping Banjo might visit me in my sleep to offer some guidance.

I woke on the morning of my birthday feeling excited with anticipation and started to help my children (May then 11, Martha 9 and Enoch 8) get ready for the day and for school. Then I looked at the map of where Fox Studios was and started to get ready for my errand. Enoch was the last out of bed this morning so I went into his room and sat next to him and sang a morning prayer. He opened his eyes (I think he was pretending to sleep) and said in a croaky voice, "Dad, I don't feel well." I knew he had been having a problem with some bullying at school. For a moment I felt a bit sad and selfish, inwardly I thought, "My son can't be sick today!" I paused and then said, "You can stay home with me today." He immediately looked cheerful and said "Yay!" and hugged me. After I finished getting May and Martha to school I turned to Enoch, "Guess what? You and I are going to Fox Studios today!" He let out an even bigger "YAY!"

---

[3] 'Abdu'l-Bahá, *'Abdu'l-Bahá' in London*, UK Bahá'í Publishing Trust, 1982, p96.

I got my copy of *Wisdom Man* and we drove to Fox Studios, Sydney, Australia, which I found was about 25 minutes from home, towards the Olympic Stadium. I pulled the car into one of the parking levels and we started walking. I had never been here before. There was a combination of tourist-type stores and office buildings. There were some extras having brunch during a break for making what might have been a period type movie. The smell of some beautiful grilled food drifted past our noses and Enoch said, "I'm hungry!" We walked over to one of the food stalls where a woman wearing something that looked like traditional Turkish clothes was making gözleme, a traditional savoury Turkish flatbread and pastry dish. It was delicious. (For years to come Enoch remembered this food as his favourite and would ask for us to return.) We walked along eating our hot gözleme and looking for where Phil Noyce's office might be.

At one point Enoch shouted, "Toy store!" and he ran off towards a brightly-lettered building. I called his name asking him to stay closer to me but he ran faster and disappeared into the store. I went in after him and saw it wasn't a toy store but a large children's clothing store. Before me was a sea of clothing racks and no sign of my son. I started to feel a bit anxious. I called out his name and started to look for him under and between the clothing racks. As I passed the shop counter a woman there who I noticed was very pregnant turned to me and said, "Can I help you?" and I quickly said, "No thank you, I'm looking for my son."

I eventually found Enoch hiding and giggling in the middle of a circular clothing rack hugging the central pole. I took his hand and we started to head out of the store. As we passed the pregnant woman behind the counter I had the thought "Well she did ask if she could help …" and so I went over to her. Again, "How can I help you?" and I said, "Would you by chance know where Phil Noyce's office is located?" Her eyebrows went up with surprise and she spoke with intense interest, "Why do you want to know where Phil Noyce's office is?" I thought to myself, "Why are you asking me like that?" but instead I started to tell her about the life of Banjo and his great compassion, wisdom and forgiveness. As I spoke her eyes started to brim with tears. I asked her what was meaningful for her in hearing about Banjo's life.

Her reply stunned me.

"In my life right now forgiveness is a powerful theme and hearing about his story has meant a great deal to me and given me hope. I also am due to give birth next week and I haven't worked here for some weeks now. I came in only today to help out a friend as a special favour. I also just graduated with my Masters in Cinematography and my thesis was on comparing Aboriginal and non-Aboriginal portrayals of biography in film. I am also a script writer." And tears streamed down her face. I was filled with wonder and joy and I said, "Wait here" (as if she was going anywhere!) and I ran with my son to a bookstore just across the lane and found they had copies of *Wisdom Man*. I bought a copy and brought it back to the store and handed it to her. "Here this is a gift for you. I am certain that I must have come here to actually find you and you are meant to be the scriptwriter. I'm sure Camilla will feel that way too and I'll put you in touch with her." I can't remember exactly all that she said in response. I do remember she expressed joy and gratitude and wonder and she said, "I would love to!" I said to her "I'll bet the whole reason we came here today was to meet you."

As Enoch and I walked away from the toy store I looked at him and thought about what a special child he was and that children are more open to the promptings of the spirit in general. I felt so glad that I hadn't chosen resentment when he asked to stay home from school. He was my little Angel for the day, who Banjo was able to guide. I told him, "You were very helpful today, you listened to the Angels and led us to meet Jane who is going to help Banjo do some important work." "Really?!" and he paused, "Where are we going now?" "To find Phil Noyce the movie director to give him *Wisdom Man*. We're making a movie!" We followed Jane Cole's directions (the clerk/mother/script writer) to the other side of Fox Studios. We got to the security guard at the gate and he called Phil's office. They told us that Phil was in South Africa filming a movie about apartheid called *Catch a Fire*.[4] I prayed for detachment around the timing of things, and comforted myself with hoping that my service to Banjo and Camilla was in finding Jane.

I went home and called Camilla and she was very happy to hear the news about Jane and gave me permission to put them in touch with each other. I still wondered how I would be able to get *Wisdom Man* to Phil but I accepted it was out of my control for now.

Several weeks later I received a text on my phone from Jane and it was all in uppercase letters. "CHRIS! YOU WON'T BELIEVE IT! I HAD MY BABY AND THE DOULA THEY SENT TO HELP ME IS THE NEXT-DOOR NEIGHBOUR TO PHIL NOYCE! I WILL GIVE HER MY COPY OF *WISDOM MAN* AND SHE WILL GIVE IT TO HIM!" I gave a whoop of joy and after googling 'doula', ran over to Enoch and told him the news. His eyes went wide with wonder "WOW!" I called Jane and she excitedly explained the details that the person sent to help her care for her newborn lived in an apartment building and the next unit over was the one Phil Noyce lived in. Jane was also filled with wonder and excitement. She said she would get back to me to share the news of how it went

4 Studio Canal, 2006

afterwards.

Some weeks passed and I began to wonder about what was happening. I said some prayers and got the guidance that each person has their own role to play and that I can't worry or try to control how or when or if they play their part. After a few months I said some more prayers and got the feeling "It is time." So I wrote an email to Jane. I decided to keep it low key and to ask her how she was and how her baby was doing. I sent the email and one day passed, and then a second day.

On the third day I received an email from her. "Chris! I'm sorry I didn't get back in touch with you. I felt so sad because I had gotten busy with taking care of my baby and I didn't end up giving *Wisdom Man* to my doula and then she left and I called the agency and they said she had moved overseas and didn't have her details. I felt so sad. And then your email came and THE NEXT NIGHT I WENT TO AN AUSTRALIAN DIRECTORS' GUILD AWARD NIGHT AND PHIL NOYCE WAS THERE! LAST NIGHT I WENT TO IT AND I MET HIM AND GAVE HIM *WISDOM MAN* AND HE SAID HE WAS INTERESTED AND WOULD READ IT!"

I called Camilla straight away and told her what had happened and then I said, "It feels like I've completed what I was meant to do. The script writer and director have been brought together and what I needed to do is complete." As I finished speaking those words I heard Camilla draw in her breath suddenly. I asked, "What is it?" She said, "As you were speaking I was standing at my kitchen window looking out and a large white bird landed on a branch outside, then a rainbow appeared over the bird and when you finished speaking the bird flew off." "That's amazing!" Then Camilla said, "Many people called Banjo 'Rainbow Man'".

Ten years later, in 2015, I was sitting outside in the late evening with Banjo's grandson, John Clarke, and I shared this story with him. When I finished he said, "I can tell you about the mystery of that white bird. Pop [Banjo] and I used to sit near the spot where he is buried now, overlooking the stream and valley. When we sat there together a white goshawk flew up and landed on a branch near us. Each time we sat together that white goshawk would fly to that branch near us. Some years later, after Pop had passed away, I went back to that spot to have a visit. That original white goshawk would have died some time back, not having that long a lifespan. Yet another white goshawk flew up to the same branch and sat with me. I thought to myself, "That's him."

Chapter 3

William Cooper

Champion of Human Rights

for the Jews

On September 25th, 2012 I was in the Wurundjeri Aboriginal Elders Council office at the Abbotsford Convent in Melbourne, Australia. One of the Elders showed me a newspaper article that was quite ill in spirit in the way it spoke about Aboriginal Elders in the community. Shortly afterwards, I spoke with Stephen Fiyalko, the CEO of the Council, who indicated they wanted to find a pro bono lawyer to assist with approaching the newspaper to retract or apologise, as the article was potentially defamatory. I saw that, combined with the negative content, placed just above that article was a large photo of a great white shark leaping out of the ocean to catch a seal between its teeth. Surely the photo inspiring fear and negative emotions placed just above the negative article about Aboriginal Elders was not lost on the editors of the paper. It wasn't lost on me.

I had only recently moved to Melbourne and so I didn't know anyone in the legal community and was at a loss as to how I might find a suitable lawyer for them. I meditated and decided to call Sam Altman (a dear friend and the Coordinator of the Bachelor of Community Management, Indigenous Studies, Macquarie University) in Sydney. He seems to be connected with everyone in Australia through two degrees of separation at most.

When I explained the situation, Sam suggested two things. The first was that I contact a friend of his who is a lawyer in Melbourne who might be willing to help.[1] He also suggested that I should contact the Jewish community to see if there might be legal help there. I asked why and Sam replied, "Because they have a long memory." I asked what that meant, he said, "They remember William Cooper." I asked who William Cooper was and Sam began to tell me one of the most amazing stories I have ever heard.

---

1   When I called this lawyer he said that coincidently he had just been thinking about Sam and doing some reading about something that had meaning for his friendship with Sam. He said he would be happy to help. I sent a copy of the article to this lawyer and put him in touch with the CEO of Wurundjeri.

On November 10, 1938, in Nazi Germany, Kristallnacht, or the 'night of broken glass' occurred. It was the beginning of the Holocaust. In Berlin over 30,000 Jews were rounded up and put into concentration camps. Many died that night. It was the night when more than 7,000 Jewish-owned shops and hundreds of Synagogues had their windows smashed and many were set on fire.

Responses from around the world varied. It is difficult to find clear and unambiguous non-Jewish responses where words and actions match. For example *The New York Times* printed an article about the night, but failed to name it for what it was, saying that the purpose of the violence was to 'make a profit for itself out of legalized loot.' U.S. President Roosevelt recalled his Ambassador to Germany for 'consultations' for ten days and verbally condemned that night. However, he did not cut off diplomatic relations with Germany and failed to support increased immigration numbers to allow Jews safe haven.

Just prior to Kristallnacht, the Australian delegate to the Intergovernmental Conference on Refugees in Evian spoke against allowing Jewish refugees to settle in Australia. He declared, "as we have no real racial problem, we are not desirous of importing one…"[2] Less than 200 Jewish children made it into Australia before war broke

---

2 Thomas Walter White, Speech Transcript, http://ergo.slv.vic.gov.au/explore-history/australia-wwii/abroad-wwii/holocaust Accessed, 25 March, 2016.

out and all immigration ceased.

One German newspaper's response summed up the significance of this international apathy, claiming justification for Kristallnacht and the Holocaust that followed. 'We can see that one likes to pity the Jews ... but no state is prepared to ... accept a few thousand Jews. Thus the conference serves to justify Germany's policy against Jewry.'

In the face of this international apathy one man's words and actions, which spoke for truth and justice contrasted brightly.[3] In December 1938, William Cooper, an Aboriginal Elder of the Yorta Yorta Nation, aged over 70, wrote a letter to the German government and led a march of Aboriginal community members to the German Consulate to protest and deliver that letter. The consulate would not open its doors to William.

Learning of this from Sam, I now understood why he suggested I approach the Jewish community to find a lawyer for the Aboriginal community: 'they have a long memory'. They remember William Cooper stood up and marched for them when no one else did. I later found out that Israel has dedicated a number of trees in two

---

3   In researching this I was looking for information on William Cooper and found the Australian Dictionary of Biography: http://adb.anu.edu.au/biography/cooper-william-5773. Accessed, 25 March, 2016. Their one page summary of William Cooper's life fails to mention any of his uniquely historic contributions to defending the human rights of the Jews. I wrote to them to suggest a revision.

separate forests to William Cooper. Somehow almost no one I've spoken to in mainstream society in Australia knows who he is.

One week later I received an email from Sam that filled me with awe and wonder. He sent me a copy of a newspaper article (dated September 25, 2012) announcing 'Melbourne Jewry to celebrate Koori ties' to celebrate the life of William Cooper by inviting his grandson and family to a Sukkot Jazz event to take place at St Kilda Synagogue's Adele Southwick Hall on 4 October 2012. The Jewish community wished to express gratitude to William Cooper's family for what he did more than 70 years earlier. So I contacted Hanna Baum, the organiser of the event and asked if I could attend. We had a long enthusiastic conversation and she invited me saying she would like a journalist who will be there to interview me about my efforts to bring recognition to Aboriginal peoples for their contribution to the world's medicines. I offered to volunteer at the event. I asked if they have any Wurundjeri community members coming, considering the event is being held on their land. She wasn't sure but called around and found out apparently not. I contacted several Wurundjeri Elders and one of the youth leaders to let them know of the event and invited them however they each indicated the notice was too short and they had previous engagements. The CEO of the Elders Council, Stephen Fiyalko said he was available and I sent him the details.

I arrived at a beautiful domed Synagogue that is clearly quite old and found Hanna who asked me to act as a security guard to greet people at the gates and direct them in the right direction as they arrive. I felt a sense of déjà vu as I greeted people at the gates and guided them as I used to be a security guard at the Baháʼí World Centre in Haifa, Israel, doing similar work.

After my duty finished I started to move towards the big hall and I met Devi, the freelance journalist covering the event and she interviewed me briefly about my own work. Devi has a spirit of enthusiasm, curiosity, a sense of wonder about the human spirit as well as a clear sense of justice. She has gentleness and an ability to listen that evokes sharing in those she interviews. She asked if we could do another interview at another time, as the event was about to begin, and I agreed. I entered the large hall and there appeared to be over 100 people present. A large contingent of those present were Russian Jews. I smiled, thinking about how my great-grandfather was a Rabbi from that part of the world. One local man came over to me and we briefly chatted and he said he used to do work for Walt Disney. I remembered my Uncle John who worked as an Imagineer for Walt Disney and eventually managed the development of Disney Tokyo.

I sat towards the back of the room. I could see up at the front there was a table where the family of William Cooper, Uncle Boydie (William's grandson), Uncle Reg Blow, some other folks, and Stephen Fiyalko were sitting. I allowed myself a moment to savour the historical reality of these people gathered together to honour William Cooper a week after hearing about him for the first time. I was in a state of awe and childlike wonder.

Speeches were made by members of the Synagogue honouring the legacy of William Cooper.

For some reason my attention seemed to be most upon Uncle Reg Blow. I noticed he had a dignity and unconditional kindness for those around him. He had a healer's energy. At one point I noticed that there was someone who I am embarrassed to say I kept a distance from because of thinking an unpleasant smell came from them. Uncle Reg intentionally went and sat down next to the person and placed his hand on theirs and listened in a way that made me feel humbled in my weakness of not loving in the way he was able to so easily show. I felt he had saintliness about him, to which all should aspire.

Later in the evening he spoke with me about his role in facilitating men's healing circles and he said this would be important work for me to think about doing. We talked about our experience in working with healing in prisons and I was reminded of Trina, who worked in the Justice Department in the area of youth in prison. She had once arranged for me to do some training for youth justice workers, and later told me I should meet Uncle Reg someday. And here I was with him now. He offered me a ride to the nearest train station and we spoke some more and as he drove he talked about his work in prisons and various forms of healing work he does. I noticed his car was quite humble for someone of his stature (it was something like a 20 year old Ford Fairmont) and I felt somewhat chagrined that someone so noble was not honoured with the reciprocity that should be given to a leader like him.

I learned soon after that this was Uncle Reg's last public appearance. He left this life on December 12, 2012.

As I wrote this chapter I looked for his obituary so I could quote the exact date. I was happy to read that he has been added to the Victorian Indigenous Honour Roll of 2012 along with Uncle Banjo Clarke. I also learned that Uncle Reg Blow was at one time the head of the Aborigines Advancement League, which William Cooper had founded in the 1930s.

A few days after the event in the synagogue, October 2012, Devi, the freelance journalist contacted me and asked if we could meet to do our interview. We met at a café in the city and she interviewed me for a few hours. We talked about a range of things around my work in trying to honour Indigenous healers for their contributions to the world's health. We also talked about the Spirituality and Social Transformation class I teach. We spoke about the Indigenous concept of honouring our ancestors in the next world and the practice of prayerful service in which we anticipate their assistance. I remember we also talked about *the importance of steadfastness in the service that we feel inspired to do so that those in the spiritual realm can guide us to the right paths. Sometimes they encourage us to move in a direction that feels inspired but isn't the actual goal, because they intend us to discover something we didn't know we wanted or needed at the time. The important part is the movement with faith so that we can be guided to the goals sometimes only they can see.*

Some weeks later Devi called, "I must share some exciting news with you!" She came to our home for one of our neighbourhood potluck gatherings. Devi described for us how she tried to get her story published by a number of mainstream papers like *The Age* and *The Australian* but they declined. Only an Aboriginal newspaper was willing to print the story of William Cooper and this contribution to the world.

Within days of *The Koori Mail* printing her story, the editor contacted Devi. Devi was told that an adult descendant of William Cooper from the other side of the family wanted to get in touch with her. Apparently there was a very old book or some form of art from the Jewish community that may have been given to William Cooper before he passed away in 1941, in thanks for his efforts to protect the Jews. After reading the article in *The Koori Mail*, Mr Cooper's grandchild, who only read *The Koori Mail*, thought that this might be the time to return that gift to keep the sacred circle of reciprocity alive.

Devi further related that William Cooper's grandson, Uncle Boydie, was going to lead a re-enactment march of community members to the German Consulate to deliver his grandfather's letter which hadn't been accepted the first time seventy-four years earlier. I was stunned! Only weeks after I learned of William Cooper this historical event was to occur.

On December 6, 2012, William Cooper's grandson, Uncle Boydie, then eighty-four years old, along with other community members, now from both Aboriginal and Jewish communities, re-enacted the march and did indeed deliver the letter to the current German Honorary Consul-General in Melbourne, Michael Pearce.

William Cooper's letter read:

> We the undersigned, on behalf of the Aboriginal inhabitants of Australia, wish to have it registered on record that: We protest whole-heartedly at the cruel persecution of the Jewish people by the Nazi government in Germany. We plead that you will make it known to your government and its military leaders that this cruel persecution of their fellow citizens must be brought to an end. We respectfully request that you accept this resolution and we look forward to the news of an immediate end to these atrocities.

German Honorary Consul-General Pearce responded in kind to those gathered. He was pleased to "right the wrong" committed by his predecessor at that same location seventy-four years earlier in refusing to accept Mr Cooper's original letter. "It was undoubtedly wrong of the Consul to refuse to accept the resolution from William Cooper,

> … because it denied the responsibility of the German government for the crimes that were then being committed against the Jews.

> It was also wrong because it failed to acknowledge the courageous gesture of a people whose freedom

and rights in their own land were heavily circumscribed and whose survival remained precarious ... Some things are beyond forgiveness and reconciliation. However, it is very important for the government and the people of Germany to take every opportunity to correct past wrongs. It is therefore with deep gratitude on their behalf that I receive this letter from Uncle Boydie.

I will pass it on to the German Foreign Office in Berlin and do my best to see that it receives a prompt and sufficient response. In that I will have the support of the German Embassy in Canberra.

After he read his statement he continued, "We'll see exactly what they do respond but I think it's a strong sense from a lot of people that we've closed the circle here."

Is the circle closed here? Certainly it is the closing of an important chapter in the fulfillment of honouring William Cooper's voice of justice and compassion. But as I worked on this chapter, there were other facets of this story unfolding. I will tell you about those in the future.

Chapter 4

A Twenty Year Prayer

(Meeting His Highness)

In 1988 I was serving at the Bahá'í World Centre as a youth volunteer. While there I read many books in my spare time. One was written by Dr Ugo Giachery, who I wrote about in an earlier chapter. Dr Giachery was born in Italy. During WWII in very dangerous conditions, Dr Giachery had arranged to secure and transport marble for the building of one of the most sacred of the Bahá'í Holy Places, the Shrine of the Báb in Haifa, Israel. Dr Giachery made a lot of sacrifices and heroic efforts to obtain and safeguard the materials which were destined for a precious purpose. He wrote about these events in a book called *Shoghi Effendi: Recollections*. Throughout, there is a sense of a love of service to humanity in general and I noticed his love for the Guardian and his love for humanity. It really moved me to see someone sacrificing their own comfort, putting their own life at risk for higher ideals. I was only nineteen when I read it and it was very inspiring for me. At the time I read this book I spoke to Mr Hooper Dunbar who was a member of the International Teaching Centre at the Bahá'í World Centre at the time. I mentioned that I had just read this eye opening book by Dr Giachery, and how much it had moved me. He responded, "Write to him, write him a letter and let him know how much this book meant to you. He's getting on, but I'm sure he would appreciate hearing that his words had moved you so. But when you write him make sure you let him know that he doesn't need to write you back because he's quite ill and frail. It would be good not to have any expectations of him writing you back. Just let him know that you want to express your appreciation."

So I did that, I wrote Dr Giachery a letter, and I was grateful to Mr Dunbar for suggesting I could. After about a month I received one of those envelopes that says 'Par Avion', one of those old style envelopes that maybe had been kept in a drawer for a long time. And inside was a piece of paper that was like translucent parchment. I hadn't seen paper like that before. There was a handwritten note going diagonally from one corner of the paper to the other. I was surprised to see that it was in Dr Giachery's own hand. I believe he was in his late eighties at the time and he was writing from his hospital bed. He had an assistant who would write things for him if he needed but he wrote this himself. That in itself ... it didn't so much matter what he said, just the fact that he had done that moved me.

But what he said in the letter was very affectionate and loving. He was full of encouragement. Just as in his book, he wrote about love for service to humanity that filled his heart. That would someday fill my heart. He wrote to me in the way that a grandfather might speak to a grandson. I've kept that letter all these years. He passed away only a few months after that so I was very blessed to have received that letter and its message from him.

Fast-forward to 2005, where, as I mentioned in chapter one, I had opened a random page of a random book looking for guidance. Within a bigger anthology I chanced to find a brief biography about Dr Giachery's life. It described that at one point Dr Giachery had gone on to Samoa and met with the Head of State, His Highness Malietoa Tanumafili II. Dr Giachery had been able to be of service to His Highness and to the Samoan people. In fact, Dr Giachery so loved Samoa that he asked to be buried there. He went there to die.

He wrote to me from Samoa. He went to the Other Side Camp from Samoa.

I would often fantasise that someday maybe I could go to Samoa and do something of service for Malietoa; for the King of Samoa. (I later found out that although people from outside countries call him a king, that's not a culturally accurate depiction of his role.) It felt like a silly bit of wish. What could I do? Just to do something that would bring Dr Giachary joy in the next world? I put that away as one of those vague longings that each of us has from time to time that doesn't necessarily happen.

In 2007 His Highness Malietoa Tanumafili II passed away. He was the longest serving monarch in the history of humanity at the time of his passing. When he went to the spiritual realm a new Head of State was appointed. I thought to myself, "Oh there is a new king. Maybe I could meet him. I don't know how, but maybe I could do some kind of service for Samoa." Again, a childish hope.

Meanwhile I was working at my PhD, *the Protection of Indigenous Medical Knowledge*. Some months later I sent one of the chapters to a Māori scientist, Marie Roberts. The chapter explored possible ways to honour the spiritual dimension of Indigenous Knowledge within Western law. I asked her for feedback and advice. Ms Roberts read it and replied, Would I be interested in presenting at an international conference sponsored by UNESCO on the Universal Declaration on Bioethics and Human Rights, which was being held in Samoa?

A few days before the conference I was told that I had been uninvited to present at the conference because this was only for Indigenous people from around the Pacific to express their concerns about the Declaration, discussing whether it should be implemented for the Pacific.

So there I was wrestling with my own ego again. Initially there had been excitement about my attending, but some of the local organisers decided that a non-Indigenous person shouldn't be speaking. And that actually made sense. There should be the Indigenous voices consulting together about this for the first time. In fact one of the main problems with these kinds of international gatherings is that Western voices dominate the Indigenous voices. I appreciated that this fact was important. It still was hard for me personally. I tried to completely let go of that want. I recognised that this was truly just a test of my *own* ego. "Oh hello ego." I said some prayers, meditated and saw that this was actually an opportunity instead of talking, to listen. Listen to the Pacific, so to speak. Listen to hear Indigenous voices of the Pacific. Because I hadn't really travelled. Other than

New Zealand, I hadn't really travelled around the Pacific or understood any of the kind of Island needs, concerns, gifts or wisdom. The more I reflected, the more it made sense - you can't talk and listen at the same time. So I just need to listen when I go there. I am a visitor. If I want to be of service to Samoa somehow I need to understand what Samoa, for example, is about.

So I attended as a participant, not a presenter. When I saw a draft of the conference program I got really excited. It said that the new Head of State, His Highness Tui Atua Tupua Tamasese Ta'isi Tupuola Tufuga Efi, the new King, (as I would have referred to him then), was opening the conference. He was going to speak! I was going to get a chance to listen to him!

We all gathered together at the venue. There were people from around the Pacific and different parts of the world. His Highness arrived with a convoy of vehicles, stepped out of a car wearing his traditional robes. That's how my Western mind would have named it. Because I didn't know the appropriate terms for the type of regalia he was wearing. But he was so dignified - royal. He was obviously worthy of veneration. Before even speaking, his bearing and the way he carried himself made me feel great admiration.

When he spoke I remember feeling really amazed because I'd never heard a Head of State speak so intelligently and cogently about traditional knowledge drawing parallels with Western scientific knowledge. Here was a Head of State quoting Stephen Hawking, referencing quantum physics, describing a resonance with *Fa'a Samoa*: the Samoan way of thinking. He expounded on the parallels and depths of knowledge between both systems that resonate with each other. It was a very deep presentation full of *'Irfān* – knowledge, awareness, understanding.

He spoke about the importance of humility for both scientists and those in traditional knowledge systems. You have to have humility in order to appreciate the sacred. Without that humility one cannot sense the sacred; or elegance of design in creation, which is a perspective required for any great scientist or traditional knowledge holder.

I was just really blown away by the beauty and wisdom of his presentation. I remember comparing him in my thoughts to other leaders around the world at the time. There was just no comparison to any I'd heard.

Afterwards he was mingling, talking with some VIPs. I saw he was speaking to a man from New Zealand. And I was kind of psyching myself up, trying to say "Okay, I'll think of something really intelligent to say. I'll walk over to the Head of State and I'm going to say something that's so meaningful that he'll notice me. And it will all just work out!"

I waited until I saw that their conversation had finished and I rushed over and I started to speak to His Highness. I can't remember what I said but I got about six words out of my mouth and then I looked to my right at the man from New Zealand and I looked at His Highness and I realised that that was just a pause in their speaking. They were still having a conversation; I had just interrupted them.

I felt my face redden. I was embarrassed and ashamed. I apologised and kind of backed away from having interrupted the Head of State and this man. As I moved away I profusely apologised to my ancestors for my arrogance in assuming I could do anything of use for this brilliant man. And just felt really embarrassed. I kept apologising in my heart and mind.

The next day, conference attendees were invited to meditate on a question posed by His Highness the day before. Although UNESCO had chosen a point of focus, the chair of the conference reminded us that His Highness had asked us to contemplate, "how do we know what is good?" It's a very simple question but when we thought about it - and these were professors and people who had done a lot of writing and thinking, just that very simple question was quite a challenge. So we were set to participate in a workshop to consider this question together.

We were grouped by table and where I had been sitting there were about five of us. Our large table seemed mostly empty. All the other tables had twelve to fourteen people. I noticed they had VIPs from the head of UNESCO and the UN, as well as proficient professors and various dignitaries from other Pacific nations.

I started saying to the four other people at the table, maybe we should break up and each go to one of the tables where the bigwigs were. A Māori grandmother is sitting there. She said, "No this is good, we'll have a small table, we'll have a good intimate conversation. We'll have some good conversations here." I said okay. We'll sit here. We were just starting to talk when in my peripheral vision I saw somebody coming up the stairs. He wore a hat. It was His Highness, in regular clothes, different from his official attire from the day before. It wasn't an official part of the program for him to be there, he just wanted to come and participate. I saw his eyes scan the full tables, then look at ours. He came over and he sat down next to me.

I was stunned. Inside I was saying to anyone in the next world who was with me, What do I do? Don't want to muck this up. The response, "Just listen." So I just listened! His Highness talked about when he was a child and he reached a milestone in his learning, his family and community would celebrate by going into the rainforest and gathering special flowers and making a special necklace, a *lai* for him to wear. The fragrance of those particular flowers would remind him of the love from the community and what he had learned or had gone through in his life at that transition period. Fragrance was such an important part of growing as a person, in remembering that your community loves you; in your growth as a human being.

At the time when he was speaking he was using a lot of cultural words. To be honest, I didn't understand about fifty percent of what he was saying. Even on the level of actual words and their meaning. So I was missing a lot of what he was saying and it was only over the next year, when reading his papers or books, that I started to replay in my mind what I'd heard from him and understand what he said. At the time though, I was not understanding a lot of what he was saying. But I appreciated that there was a deep resonance between intimacy of relationships and family, with the learning that results in some deep philosophical understanding; beyond books or abstract learning at a university. And intimate social relationships are woven with the fragrance of these flowers. It was such a beautiful concept.

Then others around the table shared their stories and I was still listening. By the end of everyone speaking, the Māori grandmother said, "Chris would you like to share something?" And I thought inside, 'What can I share that would be of use to His Highness or to the people of Samoa?' I found myself relating a story about something that happened when I was doing my PhD.

At the beginning of my PhD I had been investigating how universities around the world were researching Indigenous medical knowledge; many universities were trying to develop new medicines from Indigenous communities' knowledge, which was sometimes appropriated by multinationals in the research process. When I discovered this I felt quite concerned. When I discovered later that it was happening in my own university I was even more concerned. It was no longer something happening way out there in the big world it was actually happening where I studied. In my 'world.'

Sometime in 2001, I spoke to one of my PhD supervisors, Terry Widders, who was the only Aboriginal lecturer at Macquarie University at the time. I told him, I understand this is happening. I am new in my work, but I know enough about law to know that the law actually won't protect that Indigenous knowledge. Yet these researchers in our university are researching it. It may end up with that Indigenous community's loss of ownership and right to use their own knowledge. Terry said "Well, ask them to stop." And I was like … uh, what?

My mind was racing. I had just started my PhD. I was a new student. I'm going to speak to these professors and ask them to stop their research and like, but, I mean are they even going to listen to me? To Terry I said, "Okay. Well, I'll go and speak to them."

I contacted them by email, "My name is Chris. I'm doing my PhD in law on this subject; would love to have a meeting." They wrote back very enthusiastic. "Oh Chris, yes we know about you. In fact you're in one of our posters that we presented." I was like … what?

Evidently it's not unusual in a research application to just list the strengths of your university in order to demonstrate that it should be the institution to win grants. I had been named even though I hadn't been consulted. They told me that there was no other PhD candidate in the country working on protection of Indigenous medical knowledge, so it was quite useful for their research and they were hoping to expand a working relationship with me.

We met and I explained that they needed to stop the research at the moment because the law doesn't protect the Indigenous medical knowledge. They said, "But that's what you do. You'll protect it. You're doing your PhD and you'll figure out a way to protect it and it'll be safe." "No. I am ignorant, I don't know enough. I just know enough to know that it can't be protected at this stage. What I could do is organise a workshop where people like Terry Janke who is an Aboriginal lawyer and other Indigenous community members who've experienced this kind of thing before could all come together and we could consult and maybe there could be a solution that could be developed from that. I'd be happy to help in organising something like that. And then maybe if a solution develops from that, the research can then continue. But until then it needs to pause."

I was hoping that had gotten through, and they said "Okay that's great. We love workshops. In fact next Monday we're having a meeting with the Vice-Chancellor of the university and we're applying for half a million dollars to do more of this research. Would you come along?" To myself I thought, wait a minute, did they not hear what I just said?

I agreed to attend with some conditions. I asked them to make it clear to the Vice-Chancellor that I'm not part of the research group. I'm only there as an observer and I'd report back to the Department of Indigenous Studies anything I heard in the meeting. If they were okay with that I'd come. They agreed.

As the meeting progressed, it was clear that the Deputy Vice Chancellor wasn't going to approve the proposed grant on medical research based on Indigenous knowledge. It failed to meet the requirements of the grant to which they applied, for innovative research. Theirs needed to be a new kind of research that produced research in a new way. The idea of approaching Indigenous communities to find cancer drugs wasn't new. The Vice-Chancellor conveyed, "there are a lot of universities doing this. I don't know how this is innovative." One could see he was about to say "no." I think the researchers in the room were beginning to kind of panic.

One of them said my name and asked me to speak. And I was like, wait a minute. I'm actually supposed to be stopping this. Why has this meeting been turned over to me? I went through in my mind what I might say, and what the consequence could be. If I say this, this will happen. If I say that, that will happen. The room sort of froze as I worked through it in my heart and mind.

Something clicked. I found myself saying, "An innovative research grant is something that you hope will make the university famous and attract research in that area. If you want to be famous in the area of researching Indigenous medical knowledge you need to be the first university to be trustworthy with Indigenous communities. Because no university is trustworthy in their practice with Indigenous communities from the perspective and experience of Indigenous peoples. If you prove yourself trustworthy and allow for Indigenous communities to control the research, and determine how they want that research used, then you can go forward.

"It means turning the research over to those communities, and if you do that, the verbal network will share that this is a university that is actually trustworthy. You'll get a lot of people who will want to work with you."

"But if you end up doing it in an untrustworthy way, they will also speak with all the other communities, and no one will want to work with you. So that's the kind of choice you have in front of you.

"And, no one's ever talked about a pharmaceutical company owned by Indigenous people even though most of the world's medicines come from Indigenous people. You could actually consult with the Indigenous communities and ask them do they want to have their own pharmaceutical company and help with capacity building in that way and they could apply their own spiritual customary laws to that. And develop it in their own way."

So after, I don't know how long, the Vice-Chancellor said, "You know, I'm not going to give the $500,000 Innovative Grant for this project. But I will give you $100,000 to start a Vice-Chancellor's project on a trustworthy model of research with Indigenous peoples."

The meeting ended and we walked out and the scientists were looking at me and said, "What just happened in there?" I actually didn't really understand what had happened. I thought my contribution was over; I started to get on my bicycle to ride to class. "Chris, you need to write this grant." "What?" "Yes, this is an area around ethics and law. It's not around science. You need to be the one to write this grant application." And I'm like "I don't even know what a grant is. I've never seen one." They said, "Well you'd better learn because that's what he's asked for."

So I had to figure out how. I went to my desk and typed into Google "How to write a grant" and started reading the guides that came up. The scientists then got together with me and we basically agreed that there is no right model for protecting Indigenous medical knowledge, so what we need to do is actually engage in a process of humility where the Indigenous community is invited into conversations about what is important for protection, from their perspective and their understanding; then design something that responds to those concerns. You have to have a process of humility when you don't know the model ahead of time in the research, then you design a research process that invites consultation to create the model.

So that's what we did and the projects stemming from that ended up winning a Vice-Chancellor award, and were short-listed for the Eureka prize in Australia for communication and science.

So I'm telling this story to His Highness and those present at the table in the conference, relating to the question, how do we know something is good. Then I also remembered, "I'm not from here, but I know that in Samoa there is the Mamala Tree and that a Mormon missionary came to this country who was also an ethno-botanist; the missionary discovered that this plant had a powerful effect against HIV and asked if he could have a partnership with Samoa for this plant to be developed into a pharmaceutical drug. The response from Samoa was, "we will give this as a gift to humanity. We'll give this gift for those who are suffering from HIV. But whatever pharmaceutical company develops this, they have to promise that they will make this drug available for free, or at cost, to countries affected by the HIV epidemic. That is our condition.""

I reflected, this was not some act of random kindness. It is an actual customary law of the Samoan people, and it's a customary law of

Indigenous people around the world. Medicine is for healing. So I thought aloud, "can you imagine what the world would look like if we honoured the compassion and wisdom of Samoan and Indigenous customary law around medicine? It would transform the entire world's medical system?" His Highness didn't say anything but he smiled with wisdom.

Afterwards, through prayers and meditation, I quickly decided that the best way I could be of service to him would be to complete my PhD. I wrote it that week in Samoa. The conclusion of my PhD I wrote in Samoa, the week after meeting His Highness. I was inspired. From having listened to His Highness I recognised that the contributions of Samoan and Indigenous Customary Law could transform the global health system. That became the heart of my thesis' conclusion.

I then sent parts of my thesis to other people who had influenced and inspired me with the work. Did I quote them in the right way? Could they correct my mistakes or give feedback? A few months later I sent the conclusion to some of the participants who had sat with me at that table during the international conference on the Universal Declaration on Bioethics and Human Rights. But not to His Highness. Not yet. I had a sense that I should wait and present the whole dissertation. That might be my act of service to him. Or first act of service.

During those months I was working as a security guard at a high school in Sydney. Just before going to work, I perused an email from someone whose name I didn't recognise, inviting me to Samoa, saying that some other person whose name I didn't recognise, *Tupua*, "has asked if you would come back to Samoa and speak on a panel about some water issues in the Pacific." I was perplexed. At work, the Vice-Principal of the school happened to be working in his office. I explained the email and asked if I could briefly go online to figure out who this person was. I just needed to Google the name of the person who had asked me to come. I typed in *Tupua*, and saw that it was a shorted version of the name of the Head of State of Samoa. I turned to the Vice-Principal as it sank in, "THAT'S the KING!" I then danced around the room.

Only a month later in 2008, I flew back to Samoa with a copy of my PhD, printed out and bound in leather. It was my gift to His Highness. When I went to his house and opened the door, there before me, directly in front of the door was his bookshelf. I spotted a big folder that said Kavelin on it. And I asked, "why does it say Kavelin there?" He responded, "It's your PhD. Somebody sent it to me and I printed it out. And I've already bound it there."

When I went inside His Highness kindly asked me to tell him a bit about myself. I proceeded to tell him about my work as a security guard and we talked about that for a short while. As it was near midnight we finished speaking and I started to make my way to the place I was staying. As I left his home I thought to myself, "So after all this time, you finally get an audience with His Highness and when he gives you the chance to talk about anything, you talk about what it's like to be a security guard for fifteen minutes." I felt pretty embarrassed. Then a sweet thought, like some angel's voice, reassured me, "You don't need to worry about that. He read your PhD, he knows what's important to you. You'll be back."

As I walked in the night air I remembered that this all began with wanting to honour Dr Giachery. To do something of meaning and service for Samoa to honour Dr Giachery in the hope that it would bring him some joy in the next world.

That was how I first met His Highness Tupua Tui Atua Tupua Tamasese Ta'isi Tupuola Tufuga Efi.

Chapter 5

Diary of Third Meeting with His Highness

On January 2009 I returned for my third trip to Samoa. This was full of many blessings and I am grateful to God for all of these. To recap, during my first trip I was able to meet Samoa and to practise my listening skills with humility. This occurred in November 2007. While I was there for that first journey, I finished the last chapter of my doctoral thesis. In February 2008 someone sent my completed PhD to His Highness Tui Atua Tupua Tamasese Ta'isi Tupuola Tufuga Efi, the Head of State of Samoa, and he himself invited and arranged for me to fly to Samoa to speak. This third visit took place because His Highness permitted me to meet some family members, possibly to do work for the Samoan people. After being encouraged by His Highness, I had spent a year of working to craft a practical plan for the spiritual, social and economic development for the Pacific to be offered to His Highness. I had raised $35,000 from my school, Macquarie University in Sydney, to support the beginning of Indigenous conversations in the Pacific. My third journey in 2009 was to offer this gift and test the waters; would the people of the land feel it was appropriate? Would they want to develop this in their own way?

At the beginning of my journey as I headed to the airport I wondered what would unfold; I prayed for reliance on God's Grace, as I did not feel sufficient or worthy and was anguished that my weaknesses might delay historical possibilities for another generation. I know that while the Will of God will be done, if we fail in what we are called to do - because of our own ego, others will be raised up to achieve these purposes. But it also means the world languishes longer in the meantime. That is a heavy burden for me to consider.

A first memorable confirmation that I might be on the right track occurred as I walked from the boarding pass entry point down the ramp to the airplane; over the loudspeakers: "Blackbird singing in the dead of night, take these broken wings and learn to fly. You have always waited for this moment to arrive." I felt I was being accompanied by the beloved Guardian. I was reminded of the words to a prayer, *This is a broken-winged bird and his flight is very slow.* My beloved grandfather asked me to say that prayer when I first met with the Universal House of Justice in 1987. Also, I had sung that song in Yerrinbool Bahá'í School only a few days ago for a family talent night. I almost burst into laughter if it weren't for the tears welling up in my eyes at the feeling of spiritual embrace. From then on I felt as if my path was on holy ground and every moment my senses were heightened in anticipating purpose and guidance. I felt emptied of all knowledge and completely reliant on the Concourse on High (ancestors, spirits in the spiritual realm). That feeling of being a spiritual child stayed with me the entire trip.

When I arrived in Auckland for the transfer flight to Apia, I found that the flight was delayed by about 40 minutes due to engineering issues. I waited in the lounge and prayed and watched the faces of the mostly Samoan people filling the seats. One senior Samoan woman's face caught my attention as she listened to another senior Samoan woman whose back was to me. They were about six rows of chairs away from me. I noticed how intently she listened, how her face seemed to listen; her eyebrows would periodically lift high while her eyes performed a slow blink on the way back down as if to say: "Your voice is heard, it means something to me, I briefly close my eyes to see it inside myself." In this way she supported the importance of each thing the other woman told to her. I was mesmerised with that beauty of listening although I could not hear the sounds of the conversation held in Samoan. Later in my trip I found my own face naturally exchanging that listening ritual with Her Highness, Filia Tamasese.

I boarded the plane for Apia and found a couple who were Samoan Elders, sitting in the seats next to me. I offered the window seat to them so they wouldn't have to get up to let me in, but they deferred to me. She was the same woman whose face I had watched with wonder in the lounge. I sat down and after awhile asked them if they were visiting family or returning home and they explained they were visiting family. The husband, Rev Samu, was a Methodist minister based in Auckland although he had his ministry in Melbourne for several years before and they hoped to retire to Melbourne soon. They asked me what I was doing and about my own Faith background. I was nervous that this would end the conversation prematurely, but I am so often, thankfully, wrong about that apprehension. As I shared my story I again saw the listening expressions on her face, and with increased frequency. As though what I was saying became more interesting as the story unfolded. I spoke about my focus on the spiritual, social and legal issues surrounding Indigenous medical knowledge. Then they began to exchange words in Samoan to each other. The minister said, "What you are saying is very important to us. We have a great interest in this in our lives." But they didn't explain further.

Towards the end of the telling, the woman's eyes were glistening. They asked for my contact details, giving me a very nice pen to write them down and asking me to keep it. They said that they wanted to put their son in touch with me as he was beginning his education in health and they wanted him to get in touch with me so I could assist him on his path. I think, for those with the eyes to see it in me, a growing feeling of wonder and awe in the face of God's Grace was beginning to shine through my pores.

We landed in Samoa just after 8pm local time on January 6. There was no one to meet me at that airport, and there wasn't meant to be, but still I felt a little pang of sadness, as I love to greet others when they arrive. A taxi driver made eye contact with me. I raised my eyebrows briefly and he came over and walked me to his minivan. I asked him to drive me to the Bahá'í temple and thanked him. When I arrived in the dark, I made my way up the uneven and wet side road along the upper side of the Temple. I went to the grave of beloved Hand of the Cause, Dr Giachery and prayed. I couldn't help feeling disappointed with my own lack of feeling the appropriate emotions of gratitude suitable to the occasion ... on my first and second meeting I was spoiled with overwhelming feelings of transformation and flowing grace. When I opened my prayer book I saw the prayer Dr. Giachery had chosen for me, I wept with great joy and thankfulness. I don't recall ever reciting that prayer for myself.

> *O Thou kind Lord! From the horizon of detachment Thou hast manifested souls that, even as the shining moon, shed radiance upon the realm of heart and soul, rid themselves from the attributes of the world of existence and hastened forth unto the kingdom of immortality. With a drop from the ocean of Thy loving-kindness Thou didst oft-times moisten the gardens of their hearts until they gained incomparable freshness and beauty. The holy fragrance of Thy divine unity was diffused far and wide, shedding its sweet savours over the entire world, causing the regions of the earth to be redolent with perfume.*
>
> *Raise up then, O spirit of Purity, souls who, like those sanctified beings, will become free and pure, will adorn the world of being with a new raiment and a wondrous robe, will seek no one else but Thee, tread no path except the path of Thy good pleasure and will speak of naught but the mysteries of Thy Cause.*
>
> *O Thou kind Lord! Grant that this youth may attain unto that which is the highest aspiration of the holy ones. Endow him with the wings of Thy strengthening*

grace - wings of detachment and divine aid - that he may soar thereby into the atmosphere of Thy tender mercy, be able to partake of Thy celestial bestowals, may become a sign of divine guidance and a standard of the Concourse on High. Thou art the Potent, the Powerful, the Seeing, the Hearing.

- 'Abdu'l-Bahá

I said some more prayers and meditated further. Then I walked up the road to Steven Percival's house, a Bahá'í and Samoan *matai* (chief) who had kindly invited me to stay the night so I could say prayers in the Temple. My hotel was nearly an hour's distance on the other side of the land. He was very hospitable and we had great conversations. Steven had been a personal aide to His Highness for more than seven years. Among Steven's many roles in life, he'd often been asked by His Highness to help with a range of projects such as recording cultural performances and making documentaries.

In preparation for meeting His Highness I had been trying to read everything he had written so I could connect to his gifts and concerns. Steven gave me more of His Highness' work and I stayed up until about 1:30am reading them. Each time I read works of His Highness I feel a sense of kinship and admiration for his humility and wisdom. He has written in several diverse areas that also bring me joy ... care for those with mental health challenges, bridging the spiritual and material realms, guidance from ancestors, Indigenous law and interreligious dialogue. These are all areas of deep interest to me also but I didn't know any of our commonalities when I first felt guided to be of service to him. I'd been experiencing a growing sense of amazement that my service to him was finely designed ... no, that my very character and loves had been finely designed over many years... so that I could connect with and be of service to him in helpful ways.

At one point my heart dilated with reverence and joy as I read about the significance of 'designation.' He described that each person has a spiritual designation that they can arise to fulfil, which is unique to them, as a calling from their Creator. This meant so much more to me because Sailau, who was Deputy Director of Pacific Studies at Auckland University, had told me some weeks earlier, in reference to my desire to serve the Pacific in practical ways through what I explored in my thesis, that the Head of State told her, "It is Chris's designation." I hadn't quite understood how special that comment was until reading this part of his work.

In the morning I awoke to Steve's cat Penina Black Pearl) sitting on the bedside table staring at me. I showered and at about 7am walked down to the Temple which was then open. I said a number of prayers including my favourite prayer which speaks of angels of fire and snow, "Each day they who love Thee wake to the cup of woe because they have believed in Thee …" I chanted aloud since I was alone in the Temple. I thought of my dearest friends and felt a corresponding wave of support back to me. I prayed for the departed, my father, grandfather and others in my family. I stood up to depart, started walking and then felt a very strong spiritual tap on the shoulder, so to speak, feeling like "Haven't you forgotten someone?" Malietoa! The Bahá'í Head of State of Samoa who passed away in mid-2007. If anyone could guide me on the spiritual and cultural protocols needed for this journey it would be him! So I said a prayer for the departed, trying to focus on praying for him selflessly rather than praying for him to ask for a specific outcome or so that I could benefit personally from his guidance. It's somewhat less sincere… and then went back to the house for breakfast, which was very sincere.

While eating, Steve related his genealogy, which included connections to Tongan royalty and Hawaiian ancestors. I shared some of my own genealogy and spoke of how our ancestors meet and exchange spiritual gifts, which we benefit from. I felt reverence for our meeting.

Steve reached for the honey across the table, and it slipped out of his hand landing right side up. A spurt of honey flew in an arc into the air and landed partially across my plate and partially onto the table. We laughed and then paused looking at the design. He commented, "That is a very poetic design." I looked closely and there was a line that ran from the middle of my plate onto the middle of the table where the line became the clear shape of a fishing hook. It was the same design as the hook hanging from a necklace on Steven's own neck. I asked him what that symbolised and he said it symbolised great wealth, but not ordinary wealth. I felt again a moment of blessing had happened. The sense of wonder flared again. Was I going to have a chance to become a fisherman in that way? Would the ancestors teach me skills and give me a chance to provide abundance for others as a result of this trip? Almost too much to hope! (Steven gifted me with a handcrafted fish hook necklace four years later.)

Steven told me that His Highness had called the night before and asked Steven to bring me in the morning. I was surprised because I thought I would only see him towards the end of my trip. It was to be arranged by the two family members of His Highness, with whom I had been invited to consult on a possible project.

We went to His Highness' office and waited for him to arrive. I wasn't ready when he walked in energetically across the room. (Is one ever ready?) I had no idea how to greet him, but had no chance to figure it out as he warmly pulled me in and kissed my cheek, which I managed to reciprocate. He pressed his cheek to mine. I hadn't expected such a greeting and felt overwhelmed and undeserving. I was too stunned to remember what he said; he quickly went into his office for a meeting.

Shortly after, Steven related that His Highness had asked him to make a salad and then to go to the Royal residence for lunch at 12:30. I had been told that I was meant to see the two senior Samoan women, Kiwi, one of the most senior female Samoans in the country and Loudeen who works with her, at noon. We tried calling Kiwi and Loudeen but couldn't get through. We tried a number of times throughout the day but I later found out that the entire phone network on the Island was down for the day so it must have been meant to be ... of course. We then went to Steven's house, he made a salad and I went down and said more prayers in the Temple to prepare for the meeting. I put my gifts together for His Highness and we left and drove to his house. Steven would drop me off to catch a taxi because he had forgotten that he was to be working on news video footage for a disabled group function. He would join us at the royal residence later. I arrived at the royal house, a large house overlooking the ocean (which I found out was also the home of His previous Highness, Malietoa.) I was summoned in by Eau, a Pacific academic who was helping His Highness to edit a book.

His Highness sat in a large chair facing the centre of the room and motioned for me to sit on a couch to his right. He asked me to tell him about the project, which I had come to discuss with Kiwi. But I had some gifts for him first. I had brought two; one especially for Her Highness. The first was a Persian inlaid frame with a number of birds ornately designed in silver metal. It reminded me of the *fau*: a tree in Samoan lore that is ordinary-looking but through which the Divine speaks. I then handed him a rolled up lambskin with a painting of Layli and Majnun on it. I shared the story of Majnun seeker in *The Seven Valleys. The Seven* Valleys is a mystical work in which Bahá'u'lláh describes the stages of the soul's journey to union with the Beloved. So earnest is the ardour of his search, that at one point Majnun is seen sifting through the sand for Layli. His Highness also possessed this quality of seeking everywhere; it was obvious that he possessed an enthusiastic humility and love for the Divine. One night, the watchmen chased him, so that Majnun cursed the guards who prevented him from his searching for his beloved. He ran and ran until he scaled a wall to escape, only to find his beloved on the other side looking for a ring in the moonlight. He then realised his blessing and exclaimed that he should have praised the night watchmen from the beginning, had he known they were leading him to his heart's desire.

I told His Highness that this story reminded me of a similar story that he told in one of his papers. He wrote about accepting the injuries of discourtesy and humiliation in life with radiant acquiescence, confident that it is because we are being led towards unknown blessings, which differ from our immediate will. His Highness appeared very happy with both the gifts and stories of the gifts.

His Highness then asked me about the Indigenous conversations for the Pacific project. It involved an initial stage of having Indigenous conversations to identify spiritual values surrounding health and medicine so that an authentically Indigenous institution which reflected those values could be developed innovatively. This might enable the Pacific Indigenous voice to have integrity and equality in the globalisation process and provide for sustainable social and economic development for local communities in the full custodianship of their own medical knowledge and improvement of the health of local populations. Our conversation lasted awhile, but that sums it up pretty much.

We then had lunch. Lunch consisted of tuna steak with cream sauce over vegetables, potato wedges and Steve's salad with olive oil and crushed garlic as the dressing; fruit salad, some sweet nut and fruit loaf and coffee. It was a beautiful meal with laughter and fascinating conversations...although somehow in the back of my mind lurked feelings of inadequacy. At one point Eau asked, "what is your religion?" I began to respond, but His Highness answered, "He is Baháʼí."

Steven arrived near the end of the meal and ate while the rest of us continued speaking. When he was finished we went to the lounge; Steven took a picture of His Highness with me and we started chatting about the book that His Highness had just, that day, given to the printers. I explained how I felt when I read his work; it gave me hope; I believe that he is a consummate bridge builder whom the world needs desperately. I was surprised at how much this meant to him; he said as much. At one point I suggested he find a way for his work to reach children and illiterate people, because it is they who will benefit most from his work. As soon as the words left my lips I thought I had been too audacious and presumptuous. Yet His Highness was in complete agreement so we discussed ways that might occur.

He then asked, "Have you published your doctorate yet?" I told him I hadn't had a chance to look for a publisher. He continued saying to the other guests, "I hope he publishes it soon. I loved his work. The way he threaded through the contributions of his own ancestors and history, the clear and deep love he has for Indigenous peoples, his insight into the spiritual dimension and the translation of all of that into brilliant commentary on social analysis and solutions.... I loved it. It must be published." Steven then laughed, "I think Chris would have benefited from a video camera just now rather than a camera!" Me, "these comments will never be forgotten ..." tapping my chest with tears in my eyes.

Towards the end of our lunch meeting which ran from 12:30 to 4pm, I was feeling a sense of the importance of getting his book to the Australian public and wondered how I might help in that. All of a sudden it hit me! One of the academic contracts I had was to convene the Aboriginal Cultural Texts unit at the University of Western Sydney. I could make his book one of the course required texts! I then felt filled with excitement asked if it would be okay with him if I pursued that possibility. He was extremely happy and asked how many students would need copies. About sixty. I was, and still am, so very grateful for that inspired moment of realising a gift I could give that meant so much. I literally smacked my head as I remembered the other required textbook *Wisdom Man* by the Gunditjmara Elder Banjo Clarke as-told-to Camilla Chance. "I meant to bring a book, *Wisdom Man*, for you which I know you will love, but I will bring it as a gift the next time I am here."

One of the plain clothes police officers came into the room at the end, slightly bent over in a very humble position as he walked halfway up the room and then I noticed…..he and all the guests were not wearing any shoes…except me…! Ouch! I immediately made some kind of noise of pain or a groan and said… Was I meant to take my shoes off when I came in? I am so sorry!" They laughed and said, "Yes, but you are in good company!" pointing to the feet of His Highness who had shoes on. I managed a groaning laugh and apologised profusely. They continued to reassure me. But another good reminder of my own blindness!

His Highness arranged for the police to drive me to his other waterfront residence on the other side of the Island near my hotel where I was rescheduled to meet the senior female Elder from his family. We said goodbye and I sat in the backseat while two plain clothes police Samoan officers sat in front, and another sat next to me. I didn't know they were police officers until I asked how they came to work for His Highness. I then gave an extra sincere thank you and they gave an extra appreciative "You're welcome."

The officers dropped me off at the waterside residence of His Highness, where some relatives greeted me, offering me food or drink. I asked if they knew when Kiwi and Loudeen would; they thought possibly around 5pm.

I asked if I might have a nap on the floor of the *fale* (a traditional

Samoan structure with posts and no walls) as I'd had four hours' sleep in the past two days. The whole family began cleaning the *fale*, bringing in table cloths to decorate the surrounding tables, sweeping the floor anew, laying down mats, preparing bedding, carrying a mattress from the house and bringing in unopened new sheets still in their plastic wrapping. I felt very embarrassed. I should have just gone and laid down somewhere quietly, but my simple question imposed a necessary protocol of response on them. I experienced a pang of awareness. All I could do was thank them and at least tell them it was warm enough that I wouldn't need the top sheets so they didn't have to open them. I slept for about an hour. When I awoke Kiwi and Loudeen hadn't arrived. I asked one of the women to arrange a taxi for me to my nearby hotel as our original arrangement had been that they would call me at the hotel. Maybe they were waiting for me there. … I arrived at the hotel, the most modest I could find on the Island, unpacked and prayed and tried to be patient during the remainder of the night.

The next day Kiwi and Loudeen and I had breakfast at a fancy hotel, Aggie Grey's Lagoon Resort. The conversation went really well with jokes and deep and meaningful conversation. But I have to admit I made a bad mistake. I was asked the question, "You have to spend some time and think about the question, 'Am I doing this for myself, or am I doing this for Samoa. If the answer is yes to doing this for Samoa, then you need to learn the rhythm and pace of Samoa.'"

Instead of being attentive to the instruction, demonstrating that I understood the proper non-verbal behaviour, my naïve American side took over and I jumped to answer her question immediately. I felt very confident that I knew the answer. I explained my response in great detail. I was surprised by the resulting reaction. They seemed unhappy with what I thought was a fluent and comprehensive response. She told me there was a need for less words. Which is pretty bad because it means I was so deaf and blind to the respectful indirect allusions that it had to be voiced directly. I still didn't get it, but managed a semblance of respect and obedience.

I then stopped using extra words; I looked inward and truly tried to ask myself a question that minutes before, I thought I knew the answer to. *Palagi* (white people) are generally terrible at this practice. I managed to contemplate awhile and realised there are good reasons to be vigilant on a daily basis with one's ego (duh!) After a couple of hours I understood something I didn't before. Because Kiwi is in such a senior position and because of what is at stake in such a huge project - with huge benefits, come huge risks and potentially great damage - she HAD to ask me that question regardless of her own opinions and correspondingly I was obligated to take it seriously regardless of my own personal confidence in the resulting immediate answer. This was a question from SAMOA to me, not something for me to selfishly expound upon, or take personally and defend against as though the individual asking it thought I might be too selfish. If she had thought that, I wouldn't have been invited to consult in the first place. Instead, she could then say she had asked the question and that I had respectfully considered it and sincerely answered it. I was hit once again with self-awareness of my limited understanding. I then remembered the quote from Abdu'l-Bahá in *Some Answered Questions* about "the insistent self". The ego is so subtle and insidious that the question must be asked every day. What may have started as a selfless act can slowly (or suddenly) become a very selfish act of the ego and therefore we must ask continually, "am I doing this for others or am I doing this for me?"

The really beautiful part is, that as soon as I reached a change in my internal state, Kiwi reached out and started talking about the future of the project and how despite rhythms of consultation that were different from the Western standard, once we achieved unity things could move incredibly fast. Ironically this is faster than Western people are used to. It's the pre-unity part we have trouble with. Loudeen then commented that often in big projects, or small ones, consultation will reach a state where there are tensions and negative moments arise. It is at that time that it is most important to pause, take some time away from the conversation and anticipate the appearance of Divine intercession and be empowered to continue. I felt myself laughing with joy inside at this lesson and the certitude of seeing how these women were spiritually sensitive enough to see that I was in the right state without me speaking. Or, they were sensitive to being guided to resume important talks when I was in the right state.

The night before they had provided for me, a research paper of about ninety pages on Samoan mental health. I was to read it to help me understand their preferred methodology of consultation as well as some of the attendant Samoan spiritual values that would be important to appreciate in the project process of consultation. This paper and their continued input had been fundamental to creating New Zealand's Pacific Islander Ethical Protocols for Health Research that was produced in 2008. This was another validation that these were the right women for the job.

I have to admit another fundamental mistake on my part and another great learning moment. After breakfast Loudeen and Kiwi returned me to my hotel and left me there for the rest of the day to read their paper and reflect. I had read the first third the night before and finished, reading it slowly and carefully after a few hours which left me still with a number of hours left in the day. Ego started to take over. I felt like time was being wasted. I wasn't being paid for this trip, coming had been a great personal sacrifice. I had taken time off from work, using holiday pay, and that this seemed to be a vital, urgent project. My children really needed me at home and I should at least be making the most of this time to get work done. Why was I spending so much time sitting around instead of consulting, planning for the workshop? Were they meeting with other friends and letting me just sit here? Those thoughts are embarrassing and revealing more about my ego than truth of what was happening. I prayed to calm my busy mind and my insistent self. (I was also in for a lesson in humility regarding those immature thoughts.) I needed to say more prayers and that felt cleansing.

Loudeen picked me up in the late afternoon and drove me to the beachside house. I then had some refreshments with Kiwi and we spoke. I asked Kiwi how her day was. But before she even started to speak, the spirit answered me. I had an image of an Aboriginal Elder I knew who negotiates with CEOs of mining companies for land rights, meditates disputes between dozens of people from differing families that are very complex, has set up a women's refuge healing centre, manages it and is now setting up a youth rehabilitation centre ... all while suffering from heart disease and diabetes and movement difficulties. I then realised that Kiwi was like that and more so. Of course when Kiwi answered she explained in practical terms. When she and Loudeen had returned to Samoa from New Zealand she discovered that an historical moment had arisen. His Highness was able to return to his traditional village and they were securing funds to rebuild that village. He did this in order to encourage all Samoans to return to their villages. There had been a very destructive process of urbanisation which was damaging people's lives spiritually, culturally, materially and damaging the environment in which they lived. The women's tasks involved arranging bank loans, directing engineers and builders, networking family members' support, etc. They were doing all this at the same time as fitting in meetings with me. This was a HUGE responsibility that rested on these women's shoulders. Instead of wondering why we weren't meeting to consult more, I should have, and did realise, "I am SO lucky they are spending any time with me at all!" Hello again, humility. I'm lucky you still have the patience to visit me from time to time."

Kiwi then told me we were going to His Highness' family house for an announcement. Afterward I was allowed to take them to dinner, which I had requested earlier. When we arrived I said, "I'll just sit in the car during your family meeting so I won't intrude." They brought me in anyway. His Highness had called for the members of all his family to come so he could officially announce the rebirthing of their traditional village, which would happen in two days' time. They tried to bring me into the main room and again I tried to leave. Loudeen then asked, "as a white person, how do you have such Indigenous values? Is it because you are Baháʼí?" So we stayed out and talked on the balcony a little. We were called into the house; I couldn't avoid it any longer. We got some plastic chairs and we both sat beyond the large doorways outside the room where the family was to have their discussion.

Kiwi who sat nearest to His Highness, turned from speaking with him called me in, patting the seat right next to her. I felt very undeserving. How could I sit in that spot! I wanted to sit in the car and I was two places to the right of His Highness! I sat next to Kiwi while he gave a commanding oration in Samoan about the historical significance of what their family was doing, something that had not happened in 100 years. The oration was poetic and powerful, filled with authority and with love. I could not help but stare at the floor and listen … it did not seem appropriate to look him in the face while he spoke at this time, from his position of ancestral authority. Tears traced down my face. At some point I thought I saw someone sitting to my far right out of my peripheral vision … but no one was there when I looked. His Highness finished his speech and left the room. The rest of the family spoke in turn.

At some point Kiwi touched my arm and said Her Highness, Filia

Tamasese, was summoning me from outside the room. Her Highness took me outside the house down to the waiting car where His Highness sat in the front with his driver. They took me to a restaurant called Sails. We talked about many things, just the three of us. Kiwi and Loudeen joined us about an hour later. Her Highness is an exceptional woman of great intelligence, humour and friendliness. She has a Master's degree in Education and only recently retired from the Samoan Education Department. During the evening while sitting with His and Her Highness, I continually prayed to His Highness Malietoa asking for guidance, at one point wishing I could visit his resting place, though not knowing where it was.

At one point I was reflecting with them on the paper that Kiwi and Loudeen had given to me to read. Not only was it a good paper empirically, it reflected nearly all the same values I had. The only part that gave me pause was the idea of intergenerational curses. But when I told them this, I realised that I actually do believe it.

A few weeks after my father's passing I was saying a prayer for him. The Bahá'í Faith has a number of prayers for the departed and a common theme in all of them is forgiveness. I recalled for His and Her Highness that after I prayed for him, I heard his voice thanking me. My father said that in that forgiveness there is healing for his children and grandchildren. Through those prayers the inherited challenges are transformed into strengths and blessings.

His Highness came and sat next to me. We shared with each other some of the different ways we pray, meditate and experience guidance from our ancestors and the spiritual realm.

The next morning after breakfast Kiwi and Loudeen offered to take me around with them while they organised for the big celebrations on the following day. I got to catch a glimpse of the load of their responsibilities! There was one meeting that it seemed Loudeen wanted in private so I excused myself, asking where His Highness Malietoa's resting place was. It wasn't too far; they dropped me off. Would you believe it? In the dark of the night before I couldn't tell, but while I was speaking with His Highness at dinner, praying for Malietoa's assistance; wanting to visit him, Malietoa's resting place was about 50 meters from the restaurant. I remained there for a sweet hour and a half.

That afternoon I said goodbye to His Highness and Her Highness. I enjoyed a long conversation with Her Highness in particular. I managed to make her laugh a few times. She was telling a story and at one point used the expression, "I don't mean to get high and mighty ... "I gently interrupted her, "but you are." She paused, registered the meaning, then laughed quite loudly. She said she wished I was staying longer, that she enjoyed our conversations and she gave me gifts to take home.

In 2010 I returned to Samoa; through Kiwi and Loudeen we held simple sharing circles of traditional healers in a number of villages. There was to be no translation. No agenda other than sharing with each other in a safe space. While listening to a language I did not understand, I saw that two of the healers had tears in their eyes. Afterwards I asked if there was anything they wanted to share that was meaningful for them. One woman shared in English that her mother had taught her about a plant that healed a certain illness. She knew how to use it for that treatment, but the plant had "gone into hiding" and she could not find it any more. Another woman had replied, "my mother also taught me about that plant, but she taught me it heals something else. I did not know that it also healed what you know about. My mother gave me that plant and I have kept it alive in my garden. I can give you cuttings of that plant."

My chest welled with emotion and gratitude as I saw the immediate power of this re-birthing process.

By inviting healers to come together in a safe space to simply talk together, I witnessed the reawakening of both traditional medical knowledge and the reappearance of plants believed to be lost. How had this occurred? The legacy of colonisation and the missionary practice of labelling traditional medicine as black magic and putting it into other such derogatory categories. The traditional practices of education and social support for traditional healers were interrupted. Healers had to keep such knowledge private and pass it on within the family. Creating agenda-free, safe spaces for traditional healers to learn from each other is a key to a global revival of diverse medicines.

Chapter 6

Smokebush

Edited diary notes from December 2009:

My children were due to return from their Bahá'í pilgrimage December 5th and I longed to be in Sydney on their return. I had so wanted to be with them on that Holy journey, to companion them on their spiritual encounter with the Beloved. I could not understand why I was somehow no longer registered for that pilgrimage: it had all seemed so right. A member of the Universal House of Justice (International governing council of the Bahá'í Faith; its creation ordained by Bahá'u'lláh), Alí Nakhjavání, once told me that the first time we visit the holiest places of worship, we receive unseen blessings and spiritual gifts. The next time we visit, having utilised those blessings and gifts, we proffer our victories, which take the form of service to humanity. I had waited twenty years because I did not feel like I had anything offer. But the day I handed the Head of State of Samoa a bound copy of my PhD on the protection of Indigenous medical knowledge and transforming law to engage Indigenous spiritual concerns, I had received an invitation to pilgrimage! So it hurt and confused me that somehow was no longer allowed. I was at a loss to understand how I was no longer going on pilgrimage, my heart was heavy, and I missed my children with a deep ache.

But at least I was blessed in securing an ongoing lease in Sydney – for a room in a very spiritual home of an enlightened soul, Kali. This would provide me with a reliable safe place for respite that would allow me to spend time with my children in their familiar surroundings. I had intended to go on pilgrimage and then spend the summer with them. I arrived from New Zealand, by way of Perth, to find that the room was suddenly not going to be available. I had nowhere. I was again heartbroken, lonely and ashen. I just couldn't understand why such a beautiful reality, a simple right, a necessity for my soul - being with my children seemed riddled with difficulty and barriers. I managed to be with them for a week before our old house was due to be vacated. I was so grateful for time. I just wanted be with them; yet I could not see how I was going to find a place to stay after their move. How could I be homeless and be a present parent for my kids? All the paths in that direction seemed blocked.

That week I had lunch with Kali at the Dragonfly Café in Sydney; we mused on the mysteries of doors closing, expecting others to open. We strolled through the Eden Gardens talking about spiritual reality and the nature of light. At one point Kali noticed a bright red dragonfly caught in a large spider's web. I freed the dragonfly; gently picking the sticky spider web from its delicate wings over several minutes while Kali filmed it. While I was picking off the silvery strands, the dragonfly bit my finger, and out of surprise, I let go. She dropped; I picked her back up, finished untangling her, and off she flew with perfect grace. Kali noted that some shaman traditions say it's significant to pay attention to the symbolism of a creature that bites you. We looked it up and the first line jumped out was "The power of light". It fit with the theme of our conversation. And, Kali manages research projects in the physics department at Macquarie University that deal with light and lasers.

Later that day I found an email that had been circulated saying that Kevin Locke (a Lakota Native American) would be coming to Perth. I had just come to Sydney from Perth where I had presented a talk at a conference. In that talk I had projected in the background a painting that was in my thesis. That painting told a story of prophecy from Buffalo White Calf Woman about the unification of humanity as one family. That story I heard from a recording of Kevin's mother in 1987 when I was in Haifa and I had transcribed it for the Research Department as part of one of my jobs there. At the end of the conference in Perth I had spoken with an Aboriginal man who had attended the conference to say that I would return to connect with the Noongar people to return a medicine to them when the time seemed right.

My PhD research had followed over a number of years the trail of the development of a powerful HIV medicine that had been 'appropriated' from the Noongar people by pharmaceutical companies. Everyone in Australia had thought the trail had become a dead end when Amrad pharmaceuticals declared several years ago that it was too difficult to develop and had ceased research. However I had found out that the United States National Cancer Institute had been provided with a sample of the smokebush by a scientist at Amrad and is now working in a network of research institutions in Chicago to continue developing the AIDS drug Concurvone which came from the smokebush. I wanted to visit the local communities of the Noongar people in South-Western WA to let them know what was happening. Their knowledge is valuable to the world, even if the world is not aware of the origins.

So, when I found out Kevin Locke was visiting Perth, where I had just been, with that painting connected with that prophecy he carried, I realised it was a sign that I was meant to return much sooner than I thought. I felt I should visit Kevin first to get a sort of spiritual attunement and then travel south towards Esperance where the smokebush medical knowledge was "collected" back in the 1980's to update and return that story to the local peoples. So I bought a ticket for the next day and stayed with a dear friend and angel on earth, Dennis, who lived in a theology school above a chapel on the edge of beautiful parklands. There were wonders too numerous to recount on that two week stay.

On the day I met Kevin, the first thing I noticed was he was wearing the same T-shirt my father was wearing the last time I saw him before he passed away. It was from a Native American Bahá'í conference from 1988 in Kansas which Kevin and he both attended (though neither Kevin nor I realised this before then). I felt joy in feeling a sense of connection with my father through Kevin. I felt a combination of excited anticipation and serene trust in wanting to talk to Kevin. So much had happened since we last met in 2004 when I flew him out to speak at a conference on Indigenous Knowledge. When he saw me at the house where he was staying and was introduced to me, he gave a very relaxed, "I know Chris" and we hugged and he went on about his business in preparing for a public performance and I continued in my own meeting.

In his public performance in Perth, Kevin started with an eagle song and played a number of songs on different Northern Plains traditional flutes. He then did a hoop dance that describes the 28 days of the first moon cycle of spring using 28 hoops that add 1 hoop at each stage of the dance to show a different aspect of nature/creature. I spoke with the family Kevin was staying with and asked if I might be able to get some one-on-one time with Kevin. Kevin's mother advised that the following day they had a sweat lodge planned for him and that I was welcome to come along. I was very excited. I was asked to call her son James Bell when he arrived in Perth that night. James advised me that I wouldn't be able to come as there were too many people already going. I felt some disappointment but he advised me I could have a couple of hours with Kevin on Monday morning, the day after the sweat, which was even better if one on-one-time was what I wanted.

I also found out something that filled me with great excitement. On Tuesday Kevin was due to go south to Albany to meet with members of the Noongar community. Of course I was thrilled to see this confirmation of the inspiration to meet Kevin on my way south.

Not only was he to attune me, but he would be going to the same place I needed to go to!

One of the things I have noticed is that often crisis and victory happen internally in very sharp and immediate contrast. So when we suffer deeply over something, often something quite profound will sometimes immediately follow that illuminates our soul. So in that context… At 3:30am on Monday I received a personal phone call which was very difficult for me. I felt very sad and alone and I wept. I managed to fall back asleep for a couple of hours and then when I woke I decided to listen to Kevin's CD of music, Midnight Strong Heart which I had bought at his performance the night before.

I started reading the insert of the CD and read something that lifted me to the heights of heaven. To understand why, I need to explain some whakapapa (genealogy) of the story first. I have had three profound encounters with Ojibwe medicine people from the US and Canada. The first is that when I was 2-years-old I was given a medicine bag by an Ojibwe person. My father told me about the source of the medicine bag just before he passed away. I carried that medicine bag my whole life. The second is that during my PhD I found out about a cancer medicine called Essiac that had been appropriated from Ojibwe peoples 80 years ago and I returned that story to some Ojibwe healers whom I didn't know. The third is that a Gamiliroy Aboriginal friend of mine had visited the Ojibwe in June and returned with a sacred tobacco pouch to give me after having been told that he would know who to give it to by those Ojibwe Elders. He had let me know that to honour that gift I would need to arise in service to Indigenous peoples around the world in ways I hadn't allowed myself previously. He said a great deal was at stake.

So to return to that morning of sadness after my phone call that gave me deep grief: I had always known Kevin was Lakota from South Dakota. However as I was reading my heart thrilled to find that he is not only Lakota but also Ojibwe. His mother's father was Ojibwe, I believe. It meant a great deal to me. What mysterious connections of our ancestors above were transpiring?

After breakfast on that Monday morning I did my devotions and reflected on the spiritual quality of charity. Dennis was so kind to me. He made me breakfast and coffee each morning and was the most caring soul. He lovingly offered to take me to the meeting with Kevin. I felt that serene peace and excitement again, feeling as if I didn't even need to speak with Kevin, wishing we could just sit next to each other and pray and let our ancestors exchange gifts and stories in the spiritual realm. My dear friend Dennis drove me there and came in with me to say hello to Kevin. Kevin was waiting and right away went out to the back yard and sat at a table placing a prayer book in front of him. We talked for a bit and then I said, "Could we share some prayers?" and Kevin said, "Thank you for suggesting that Chris." I noticed the wind started blowing during one of the prayers and I was so happy in that moment feeling a deeper connection to spirit.

I had an interesting test of selfishness that morning. I had anticipated that Dennis was just going to drop me off and I was thinking "How am I going to share with Kevin all the profound things that happened since we last met and give him a sense of why I am heading south after meeting with him? How can I do it in 2 hours?" (It felt kind of like an inner child shouting "How can I get my attunement!") Dennis ended up staying to talk with Kevin. I believe he thought I had the whole day with Kevin. I listened to the anxious voice inside and prayed for detachment and wisdom. I immediately remembered my earlier meditations on the charity of Dennis, and realised profoundly that he needed this connection with Kevin and that it would be healing for him. I decided to focus on this as a gift for him and let go as best I could.

I then had another thought, "You will get much more time to speak with him when you travel south together." Now this was an internal thing and no one had told me I would be going south with Kevin, but Kevin spoke up at the next pause in conversation and said, "So you're coming to Albany with me?" Sheer delight arose in my soul. I told him I hadn't spoken with James about it yet but it would be wonderful. (He repeated that question to me at least one more time later in the day.) I have to admit even after such strong confirmations I had trouble believing. I mean I hadn't asked James yet and hadn't he reversed the offer for me to go to the sweat lodge? It might not happen still. So in the remaining 5 minutes after Dennis left I found myself still trying to share the exciting background that led to this moment of meeting Kevin. However each time I tried it was as if the sound disappeared into a vacuum… dissipating several feet after it left my mouth. It was not the time or the place. I needed to trust. The time will come.

I accompanied Kevin to his performances through the rest of the day (to schools etc.) and just listened and enjoyed the many different songs of his ancestors he shared. (I later found out he carries literally thousands of flute songs/stories and that he is the only remaining person on earth to know many of them). There were many moments of realising why I needed to listen too numerous to record here so they must be left to continue their impression on my soul.

On Monday night Kevin gave a fireside talk (a discussion of the

Baháʼí Faith). There were about 30 or so people there. I found a chair and sat down waiting for the evening to begin. I thought he might sit in the big chair in the corner so I sat on one of the wooden chairs lined up against the sliding doors. Instead of sitting where I thought he would, Kevin came over and sat in the chair to my left. I found myself watching his hands a number of times and then looking at my own hands to see that they often were mirroring his subconsciously. He turned to look me in the eyes during several profound moments in his story telling. One of the first stories he told was an Ojibwe creation story that spoke of personal sacrifice and devotion, sacrificing even ourselves for our love for others. The story spoke also of great compassion, faith and hope. At one point after one of the characters, a tiny muskrat in the story had given up his life for what he believed in to save the world, and Wisdom Woman was holding some earth in her hand praying for her hope for the world, tears began to trace down my cheek. At that point in the story Kevin said that Wisdom Woman expressed such devotion in her prayer that a single tear traced down her cheek and landed on the soil and the earth was reborn. It was so powerful, so moving. He told stories of how he became a Baháʼí by fasting a number of times and searching for the fulfillment of the prophecies of his people. It was such a beautiful night.

Afterwards while we were having refreshments he came up to me and said again, "So you're coming with me to Albany tomorrow?" I then went to see James to consult with him. He was very generous and open to that happening and told me that we would leave at 5am. (I then remembered that sometimes I have made the mistake of thinking a question is a question when it is actually a statement of reality… particularly when "asked" by an Indigenous person.)

I had given Dennis a prayer book earlier in the day and when we returned we prayed together until 1am. I then slept 3 hours, packed and caught a taxi to where Kevin was staying. I knocked on the door gently a few times but there was no answer. Perhaps I knocked too gently, but I thought in case they were still asleep I would sit on the front porch and wait. They eventually came out.

We set off to drive the 5 hour journey south and I sat in the back with Kevin's grandson, Ohitika (9yrs old). He was pretty tired leaving so early and lay against me with a pillow and slept. I had the bounty of listening to Kevin telling stories and discussing the Bahá'í writings. The sun was an unnaturally dark red as it rose in the sky and stayed that way for the first hour of our journey. This was due to smoke in the air from some forest fire in the region.

In discussing some of my work on honouring Indigenous healers and medicine Kevin asked me if I knew Linda Jones who is a professor of Ethnobotany at Sitting Bull College in South Dakota. As a matter of fact I had met her 2 years before when she travelled to Australia and we had made quite a connection. Linda had invited me to work with her to collaborate and reinforce our shared purpose but I had not yet visited Sitting Bull College. Kevin told me she is his cousin and said several times during our journey that it would be good if she and I connected again. I remembered she showed me a picture of her husband who had a T-shirt that had the "Calvin Klein" logo of "CK", but in small print with capital letters was "Custer Killer". Linda had told me her husband was a direct descendant of someone responsible for General Custer's death. I wanted to share that with Kevin and James, and each time I remembered there was other conversation happening and it wasn't until the end of the next day I managed to share the memory of that t-shirt. (They already knew of course, lol). One last thing on this thread - in the Indigenous leadership classes I would later teach in Sydney, I would remind the students that the greatest successful moments for Indigenous peoples in history were when they managed unity with each other against colonisation. I would give the defeat of General Custer as an example.

We stopped for some coffee after about an hour and a half at a small café/petrol station. I went inside to get coffees for Kevin and me. The woman inside had lovely straight black hair and told me she made the best coffees around. I noticed she had dragonfly earrings on and felt a sense of joy inside. Kevin walked in and she looked up and said, "Are you Native American?" "Yes", he answered. Her face lit up with a smile and she said excitedly, "I'm Native American too! I don't know which tribe my family comes from though." We shared some more stories for about 10 minutes and the joy was much greater than one usually receives from a cup of coffee. When we came out we told James about the Native American café owner inside and he exclaimed, "Of all the places along our journey we stop at the one place there is a Native American!" I just said, "It wasn't a coincidence. On journeys of dedicated service like this, the ancestors are the tour guides."

Kevin took over the driving and off we went. Kevin said, "She had some nice dragonfly earrings." There was a pause and then I said, "Last week I was bitten by a dragonfly." Kevin looked genuinely shocked, "It BIT you?! I didn't know dragonflies bite!" (I almost laughed because of his surprised expression.) I then told him the story of releasing the dragonfly from the spider web. There was another pause and then Kevin said, "The dragonfly was one of Chief Sitting Bull's medicines." My heart leapt in my chest and I tried to remember what I could of Sitting Bull…knowing that it must be significant, but my memory was vacant and I was too embarrassed to admit that I couldn't remember much about him. Kevin then said, "Today (December the 15th) is the anniversary of the day Sitting Bull died." I knew then that there was indeed something significant about Chief Sitting Bull, perhaps even some connection with him in the next world that warranted me to hold on to the sacredness of that until the light of it was revealed. I feel there must be a number of levels to what I am meant to learn from these connections. (On my return I have begun reading about Sitting Bull and had an "Of course!" moment in remembering he was responsible for the downfall of the 7th Cavalry and General Custer.)

We arrived in Albany and drove to Sue Martin's house. Sue had been inspired to arrange Kevin's visit with the Noongar community around Albany. We had something to drink and then moved on, as the day was very full with our first meeting almost immediately at the Noongar Centre. Some of the Elders of the Noongar community were there to meet with Kevin. An Elder, Uncle Eugene, shared stories of colonisation in Australia and the Aboriginal journey with Kevin. I was most impressed with his focus on the need for love to characterise our relationships between cultures and the incredible nobility and strength required to maintain faith in love in the face of all his people have faced. One does not see that quality maintained everywhere in the face of colonisation and it is such a beautiful light.

After the "men's business" a female Elder, (later I found her name was Carol), came in briefly and introduced herself. I did not "see" her (light) until later in the day.

We visited a local school, Mt Lockyer PS, where Kevin had been invited to perform. It was a full assembly hall. I acted as a gopher trying to keep my eyes out for what Kevin needed to get ready for his performance and afterwards.

During the performance there were a number of Aboriginal people present. One in particular was a man, Ashley White from Kalgoorlie, who was sitting, holding a didgeridoo, in one of the chairs lining the wall. I felt drawn to watch his face during the performance. As Kevin demonstrated his incredible skill in flowing through patterns of 28 hoops always maintaining the unbroken rhythm as he jumped with every beat weaving the hoops between his feet and over his body in a flow of movement too swift to see how it was done… As Kevin did this and it escaped the attention of most…the face of Ashley held appropriate awe and a depth of appreciation in witnessing the greatness of what he was seeing. I thought to myself that it was because that greatness is echoed in him.

There were moments during the other parts of the performance, in the soulful flute playing by Kevin, that tears welled up and my heart expanded to touch sacred places beyond. Ashley came up to me afterwards and asked me if it was ok if he gave Kevin the didgeridoo that he held, wanting to know if Kevin would be able to manage it on the flight. I explained that I did not know as I had only travelled with Kevin from Perth, but that Kevin's heart would be moved in appreciating the value of this gift seeing Ashley had made it himself and he should go ahead. We formed a sharing circle after the children had dispersed and some of the parents and teachers remained behind to watch him present the didgeridoo to Kevin. Kevin put it to his lips and surprisingly, or not, the sound flowed through in the ancient reverberations as if he had played before.

Ashley and another Aboriginal man, Wayne Devine, the Regional Aboriginal Education Manager, continued to show Kevin ways of playing it and the skill of circular breathing. Just after this man told Kevin in a hushed voice, "You need to make sure only men touch this. It is for men only," the female Elder, Carol walked up. (I started laughing inside seeing what was to happen.) She reached out her hand and asked, "Do you mind? I need to listen and see if there is a spirit inside." There was a pause and she asked again. The man handed her the didgeridoo and she carefully adjusted it and listened to the end you blow into. She paused, "No....wait...YES.... there is a spirit." And handed it back, going over to sit back down.

My heart was soaring in that moment. I had seen her. I needed to speak with her. I felt my ancestors urging me in her direction. I walked over to her as I saw she was rising up to leave and asked, "Carol, do you think I might have a moment with you?" and introduced myself. I started to share the story about discovering smokebush being used to develop an HIV medicine and she stopped me after only 90 seconds or so with a very excited look…. starting to speak with eagerness. "This is very, very important. We are in the middle of a big native title case and this information will help us in our appeal to the courts. Can you meet with the Land Council in our next meeting in Perth? Your work is very important and will strengthen us."

I found out later that Carol was a member of the Albany Aboriginal Corporation and that she received the 2008 Australian Female Indigenous Elder of the Year Award. Again, I didn't have time to share the full story, nor did I need to, she had connected almost immediately with the spirit of it and had seen its spiritual value. The case she mentioned I knew only a little bit about, but remembered in first hearing of it that it seemed like the largest Native Title Case since Eddie Mabo. Was it possible I might play a role, however small, in being part of the historical narrative of this case? It seemed too much to hope for, too much to dream! I had worried on the way to Albany if I would find people who were interested much less find value in what I had to bring them. My heart burst in my chest and I continued to listen as best I could, but felt I was watching from above in heaven, a scene below whose conversation muted into the background as celestial music played.

As we packed up I saw the tiredness in Kevin and he commented to me he would love a nap as he was running on pure adrenalin after having woken the night before at 2:30 am. When we got outside I didn't see James so we couldn't get into our car. I practised assertiveness and asked some friends from the area to get out of their car so that Kevin could lie down in their front seat to have a nap. They did and I put the seat down and went over to him and let him know there was a place to have a nap. He lay down and I asked everyone to stay away from the car while I packed his gear into the other car we were travelling in.

While we were waiting someone gave Ohitika five small chocolate bars. I will never forget the look on his face as he spread out the five chocolate bars and solemnly declared, "But this is too much. Five is too much." And he started handing out chocolate bars to people until he only had one and then he said, "This is right now." After about 20 minutes we all got in the cars and travelled back to the Noongar centre for a barbecue and another performance. On the way I turned to Ohitika and said, "I am very impressed with your respect and generosity. You set an example for us all. I would have trouble giving my chocolate away and I am an adult. You have taught me today. In fact if everyone in the world followed your example, there would be no more wars. If the world followed your example there would be world peace." He looked very seriously at me while I was speaking and then a sense of wonder spread across his face, "Really? Wow!"

We arrived at the Noongar Centre and people were starting to arrive for the BBQ and Kevin's performance that was hastily arranged that afternoon when it was realised that he wanted to perform for everyone. I met another Elder. When we connected he had a light in his eyes. After a few minutes of chat, during which I said I wanted to be of service to his people and had a gift, he took me outside so that just he and I could talk. I found myself surprised that every time I tried to speak about the nature of the gift I had for them he would shift the conversation. We walked some distance away from the Centre and stood in front of his truck. He looked at me with a gleam in his eye as he took out a folded piece of A4 paper and said, "Today I wrote this. I don't know why I did. But I did. Here." And he unfolded it and spread it out on the hood of his truck inviting me with his eyes to read what he had written. It was like a strategic plan and was written in blocks of writing and as my eyes swiftly drew towards one line in the middle on the right side of the page, I laughed with delight. He laughed too and said, "I know which line you are laughing at." And we laughed together. And I read out loud the line that shone in the light between our hearts. "Healing the Earth, Healing the People." There was no need to talk. There was no need to say it out loud. I was so very, very happy. My father and my uncle John laughed with me from the next world. He called out to a grandchild of his and the young man who was perhaps ten-years-old and a striking-looking beautiful human being, recited the things he had been learning from his grandfather.

What was this strategic plan, this vision he laid out before me and invited me to share with him? A Bush University of the Noongar people. We went back inside and sat down, and someone, an angel, I don't know who, stuck a laptop with photos on it in front of us. They were photos of the Bush University he was building. It was a simple design. A semi-circular meeting area with poles and walls with a thatched roof open to the centre. I looked at the roof and drew in my breath. My heart raced and I knew, even though I have never seen it before. And although I knew the answer, I wanted to hear him say it, "The material you chose to make the roof out of…is that smokebush?" "Yes. Yes it is." I wanted to burst into joyful tears right there and then. The very same plant is offering itself to the world to heal us of the AIDS epidemic, the story of which I wished to return to these people, lined the roof, WAS the roof of the Bush

University of the Noongar people just erected this year. Again... it was as if I found myself watching from heaven, and celestial music surrounded us and swelled ....making words unnecessary.

Eventually the room began to fill with people. I noticed one woman who had passed through earlier in the day and went over to her to talk. She had something like a French accent (I later found out she was a healer from the Seychelles). She commented on my energy and heart a couple of times during the night. At one point she told me, "You need to go to Arizona. There is a Native American healer there you need to meet. You need to go to Arizona." I just said, "But my work is in the Pacific at the moment." She just looked at me again and said, "You need to go to Arizona." I took it with a grain of salt but tried to respect the possibility.

Kevin did his show and you could see that a number of people were moved strongly in their hearts with some Elders with tears flowing down their faces. It was a beautiful night. I saw Ashley's wife at the meeting and felt inspired to give her my copy of Kevin's music to give to her husband as they were all sold out and I remembered the tears in his eyes as he heard Kevin. Sue and a few others commented that night that it was very significant that white (wadjella) and Indigenous (Noongar) came together in the Centre to see Kevin and it was historic.

We stayed at Margaret Mangan's house that night. She was very gracious and a loving hostess to us all. We decided to have dawn prayers at Kalgan, the place of the two rivers. We were driving along the river bank. The car in front of us held Kevin, Sue, James and Ohitika. I was with Margaret. Kevin's car slowed in front of us and stopped for a minute and Margaret exclaimed, "Look!" and pointed at the tree the car in front had stopped under. At the top were two sea eagles with proud white feathered heads. We drove a bit further and when Kevin got out I asked, "So you stopped to admire the couple?" Kevin smiled politely but clearly wasn't sure what I was referring to. I said, "The eagles. You stopped under the eagles." He looked surprised and I said "Here, look!" And ran down to the bend of the river bank which gave a view of the tree we had passed. As we looked out towards the tree, one of the pair of eagles launched itself and soared along the river and did an unusual seeming flutter of its wings, as if it was trying to imitate a hummingbird for a second, doing it a few times as it soared. Kevin was impressed.

The next day we had a meeting with the Department of Indigenous Affairs (DIA). Aunty Carol met up with us at Margaret's house and she and Kevin and I drove down and met with the most senior officer present, Harley Coyne. It was a pretty mundane meeting, but there were a couple of notable moments (because they proved to be significant later). One was when the director was describing the health care of Aboriginal people. I asked if they had midwives using traditional Aboriginal birthing practices as the Aboriginal health service, 'Congress', in Alice Springs does, and as the New Zealand government pays Māori midwives to practise Māori birthing practices. I also asked if public hospitals in the area allowed Aboriginal people to honour the practice of burying the placenta (as when I last heard, this was illegal in Queensland and I wondered what the situation was in Western Australia). Harley advised that he wasn't aware of it, and that colonisation had affected their traditional practices. I was impressed with his honesty. At another point there was discussion about how old certain sacred sites were. There was discussion about how archaeologists had proven the age of certain sites (mentioning some at 25,000 years). I found myself saying, "All this dating technology proves is how Western technology is getting better over time at recognising how ancient Indigenous civilisation really is. In 50 years' time we will exclaim, 'Look how good our technology is, it shows the Aboriginal civilization is actually 100,000 years old.' Oral traditions have been, and will always be much more accurate in describing how old they are. There are memories of sacred sites now out in the Ocean that used to be land much longer ago than that. Carol remembered that one of her stories describes a mountain that is no longer there and we held that realisation in wonder. How long would it take for a mountain to wear down? The director also commented that dingoes only showed up 6,000 years ago and had come down from the North in Asia. Kevin exclaimed surprise at that, "Our traditions always said that man and dog relationships go back to the beginning of man. How could that be?"

We left the DIA and headed off to a sacred hill where Aunty Carol shared creation stories of the local area with us. She talked about how two snake brothers wrestled over one not showing respect in providing for the family and the fight made the landmarks of the area, the islands and the bay. Part of the story included the biting in half of a dog…here Carol paused and said, "See! We were right! Our creation story includes the story of a dog. Dogs must have been here much longer ago!" Afterwards I asked if we could say some prayers together and Carol took us to a large rock. We stood on the rock and each of us said some prayers. I sang "Blessed is the spot" and everyone, including Carol, I think, joined in.

Afterwards Carol walked with me and said, "You spoke about the traditional midwives. I remember them. I remember when I was young some of them went around being sad and saying, "We can't find that bush! The bush we use for birthing medicine is gone." She said, "I wish I could find that bush, but I don't know what it looks like." I felt inspired to offer to find out for her. She said, "That would be wonderful, you could use your connections." I replied, "Actually, I can't think of any connections off hand, but the way I would do it would be to just open myself to that act of service for you and let the ancestors guide me. One way to do it would be to go to other peoples in Australia until I find ones that have their own bushes that fulfill a similar purpose. That bush would be a relative of the bush you were looking for. They might have similarities that would let us recognise it. I'll see what I can do."

We visited Albany Senior School as our last stop before returning to Perth. That was organised by Margaret James, and lunch was provided by Follow the Dream and the Great Southern Employment Development Committee (GSEDC). The school Principal attended to welcome Kevin. Our conversations were varied, but we focused on the truth of world peace.

We drove back up to Perth and I felt so very blessed to have connected with Kevin and felt gratitude to James in his generosity and openness in making room for me. One funny moment for me on the way back was I said, "Look, four generations in this car." Kevin exclaimed, "Four? I'm not that much older than you!" (Kevin I think is 55, I'm 42, James is 22 and Otihika 9). On the way back we climbed a small mountain and it was wonderful to stretch our legs. Boy, Kevin was sure in good shape! I had the lovely excuse of accompanying Otihika who wanted to walk slower as Kevin and James loped up the mountain like wolves.

Kevin suggested ways I could find to bring him out to this part of the world again so I planned to do that for November 2011. In April 2010 I planned to take a tour of the Indian reservations I used to live on in the central part of the U.S. when I was young, and also visit Kevin and Linda Jones. I was to finish my journey in Canada to repatriate the story of a cancer drug to the Tsimshian Tribe in British Columbia (I made a discovery through long investigations that the world's biggest selling cancer drug used for breast and ovarian cancer, Taxol, had significant origins from their knowledge).

In concluding, the day Kevin left I was invited to a devotional gathering at Keith and Fiona Mcdonald's house in Perth. Keith did an amazing job of choosing and timing beautiful devotional music to various writings on world peace. It was a very powerful night of the heart and connecting to the soul. I feel I could write a hundred pages trying to describe the spiritual realities experienced in those 3 hours. But one thing I must record is my meeting of a woman Sholeh Boyle. I had seen Sholeh at the first of Kevin's performances in Perth and there was something about her that made me look twice and say to myself, "Hmmmm, that's interesting." Something about her beautiful spirit. I was sharing with her about my growing up with different Native American communities. Sholeh had been previously married to a Native Cree Canadian but now lives on Vancouver Island with her husband Charles Boyle.

From her first marriage she had a daughter, Anisa White, who, Sholeh advised, was married to the newly elected Chief of the Salish people. Located where? British Columbia. That is where I was going to repatriate the cancer drug. I also realised when I heard her daughter's name that I feel called to serve her and her husband, but I am not sure in what way. Then Sholeh told me she had lived in the Pacific for a long time and that her daughter was actually born in the Solomon Islands and was more of an Islander in heart. Oh and another 'coincidence'? Laughing to myself as she shared with me that she is an expert in Indigenous public health in the Pacific. And another 'coincidence'? She is also a nurse who specialises in treating breast cancer using two drugs, Essiac and Taxol.

Chapter 7

Vaughan's Mother

On September 29, 2009 my mobile phone rang. I was in a video store in Hamilton New Zealand, looking for a Disney movie. That phone call was one of the most surreal moments of my life. It was noisy and I had trouble hearing, but I realised that the person on the other end of the phone was a dear friend, Sailau, and she was calling me from Samoa. Sailau asked how I was and then said that someone wanted to speak to me. She handed over the phone to someone and then I realised who that someone was. I found myself saying, "Yes your Highness." It was the Head of State of Samoa, His Highness Tui AtuaTupua Tamasese Ta'isi Tupuola Tufuga Efi.

I remember what day it was because the next day was when the Tsunami hit Samoa (although I almost never watch the news and didn't find out for more than a week). I think people were looking at me strangely because I kept using the phrase, "Yes your Highness". I had to decide which was less noisy, the children's section of the video store or outside where there was traffic. I went outside for privacy and did my best to listen.

His Highness was speaking about the presentation he was preparing for the Parliament of the World's Religions which was due to happen in Melbourne in two months' time[1]. During the conversation he mentioned a book about the Dalai Lama. I remembered that more than a year earlier I had once told His Highness that I felt that his mind and the mind of the Dalai Lama had a similar energy of compassion and wisdom and it would be wonderful to see them brought together to meet some day. In that moment of mental double take of "book?" I realised that this is one of the ways those in the spiritual realm work. They will give you an important thought in a way that makes you do a double take. I felt it was important to remember that earlier conversation and the idea of bringing them

---

1 Earlier in January, 2009 I had contacted the organisers of the Parliament of the World's Religions to suggest that they invite His Highness to share his wisdom and understanding of Samoan religion and thought. That invitation involved a number of conversations with the organisers and exploring how one respectfully invites a Head of State in a way that honours his *mana* (spiritual, cultural and political status).

together.

The next day I was driving through Ngaruawhahia, just north of Hamilton, and I had another phone conversation. This time it was with a dear friend in Melbourne, Vaughan Panapa. He asked where I was and I named the place. He sounded surprised and asked me for a favour: to visit the sacred Mount Taupiri where his mother is buried and say some prayers for her. I went straight away. I spent hours walking over the mountain looking for a resting place that had the name "Panapa" on it but couldn't find it. So I decided to say prayers and hope it was the right place. It didn't feel like it so I came back the next day and said prayers on the other side of the mountain. There was still no response or feeling. On the third day I went to the Eastern side of the mountain and stood to pray in a place where there was no headstone. I felt a strong desire to prostrate myself this time and my heart felt very open. I prostrated myself and offered myself in service to the land and the families of the people buried there. I felt an amazing wave of energy respond back from the whole mountain, a chorus, a wave of voices singing back to me. I wept while prostrate there.

Among those voices I could single out one feminine voice and she said, "Go and see my son. Go and see my son now." I didn't pause and I went straight home and although I only had a few hundred dollars in my account, I booked a ticket from Auckland to Melbourne to see Vaughan the next day. I called him and let him know I would be arriving after 11pm the next day. On the way there I remember becoming quite ill, developing a fever and flu. By the time I was at his house I felt quite poor physically, but we were so excited to see each other we stayed up till past 3am talking. I remember one moment where Vaughan mentioned that his mother's resting place didn't have a headstone. (I smacked my forehead internally at that point. Now you tell me! lol).

Fariba, Vaughan's wife, suggested we go to sleep and I agreed and said that I would need to go to work with Vaughan in the morning. She paused and said, "But you are ill! You need to rest! His job is in a high-rise building in the city and it takes an hour to get there. You should stay home and rest while he is at work and see him when he finishes." I didn't know why I said it, but I found myself saying, "I need to go to work with him. I don't know why." We went to bed and I fell asleep straight away. I woke three hours later feeling fresh and energetic and completely healthy, full of joy and anticipation.

After a lovely breakfast made by Fariba, we took the 40-minute bus ride to the city and continued our wonderful conversation. We arrived at his office which deals with education via the internet and he found me a chair to sit down in next to his desk. He took me around and introduced me to the staff on the floor and we sat down to do our own work. I noticed someone come in out of the corner of my eye and Vaughan said, "Oh, there is someone I need to introduce you to, she is the Director." We walked across the office and there was a beautiful woman with red hair and shining happy eyes. Vaughan then said, "May I introduce one luminescent soul to another." And then the woman said, "I lay rose petals at your feet." That's all I remember.

We walked back to Vaughan's office and as we sat down I said, "What a spiritually beautiful woman! That was the most unusual introduction I've ever had!" Vaughan paused and said, "She wears a number of hats… in fact… I think she has something to do with arranging for the Dalai Lama to visit Australia for the World Parliament of Religions." Inside I was like: "Say what?"

I turned to Vaughan and said, "I will be back. Now I know why I'm here." I immediately stood up and walked across the office. I walked up to her and explained to her what had happened up until the point of meeting her, concluding with, "And I believe I am meant to ask you to arrange a meeting between the Head of State of Samoa and the Dalai Lama." She didn't even pause and with a beautiful smile said, "I will write to his assistant now and forward it to you shortly." We laughed and then I went and sat back down in

Vaughan's office. I told Vaughan what had happened and the background of the Head of State of Samoa's phone call, which he hadn't known about. The woman came up to me within 15 minutes with a printout of the letter she had written to the Dalai Lama's assistant explaining some of the background and to expect me to contact them.

After work, we went back to Vaughan's home and let Fariba know what had happened. A friend of Vaughan's came over and we all had dinner and talked about the Bahá'í writings. At one point I said how amazing it was that Vaughan's mother had known to send me here to meet that woman. Then we talked a little about the place Vaughan's mother had come from, Ratana near Whanganui. Vaughan mentioned that there were some historical books from the turn of the previous century from Ratana[2]. He pointed to them and pulled one of the volumes out. I remember thinking they looked like the *Star of the West* series. I opened one of them and there was a bookmark in one of the pages. It was just a plain piece of paper with handwriting on it. A shopping list. I said, "There's a shopping list that's been used as a bookmark here." And I showed it to Vaughan. Vaughan said it was his mother's handwriting. My heart burst with emotion and I felt her love for him. I started to read the page out loud that she had bookmarked for us. It contained quotes

2   One of the foremost Māori prophets from around the turn of the 20th century.

from the Bible and comments about how the Angels work with us in this world to achieve victories. Clear as the light of day, here was Vaughan's mother reassuring him of her ongoing love, connection and assistance. There was an electric silence in the room and we both had tears in our eyes.

About two months later I was in Perth for a conference. On the way back to New Zealand I had to change flights in Sydney and had a couple of hours between flights. I was walking along the concourse when I saw two men wearing yellow robes standing in front of a doorway. It looked like they were waiting for someone. Instantly I knew who they were waiting for and I walked over and stood next to them. They turned and we smiled at each other. After about 10 minutes the three of us had swelled to a group and in 15 minutes to a gathering and by 20 minutes there was a crowd with police and organised lines of people on either side of a corridor for whoever this sea of saffron smiling monks was to welcome.

Then people brought out a sign "Welcome to Sydney Dalai Lama!" Even though I had a privileged spot right next to the door in front of all those people I realised I didn't need to meet him then. The time would come later if that was meant to be. My job was to say a prayer for him before he came out and let him pass through that prayer on his way into Australia. So I stood in that spot and said a few prayers including the *Remover of Difficulties* and *Blessed is the Spot* and imagined the Dalai Lama walking through the energy of those prayers as he emerged and receiving whatever blessings he needed. And then I took a picture of the crowd with the banner and then walked about a hundred metres away and sat down and had a coffee listening to the happy cheers.

Now fast-forwarding to one day in the beginning of June 2011, I was driving from a town in New Zealand, Ngaruawhahia, on the way home to Hamilton. I was meditating having recently received an email from a Native American who invited me to a ceremony in North America. I was thinking about how I had hoped to return the knowledge of a cancer medicine to their tribe and also how I had just discovered that my grandfather had spent time with that same tribe some years ago.

I turned left on the highway continuing my meditation until after about 15 minutes I rounded a corner in the highway and there in front of me was the sacred mountain Taupiri. I had gone the wrong way on the highway! I laughed and did a U-turn on the highway and as I did a voice said, "Wrong way?" I did a mental "Oh!" and did another U-turn going back towards Mt. Taupiri. I wondered why and thought, "Well, I was meditating on whether I should buy plane tickets to go to the Sundance ceremony and if I do go it would be a good idea to go to this sacred mountain (all the Māori Kings and Queens are buried there) and ask for blessings to take to the U.S. with me to share." So I went back to the area where I had prayed more than a year before when I offered myself in service. I stood there and started to pray, but before I really got going I noticed that about 40 feet away from me there was a simple wooden plank bench in front of one of the graves. I thought, "Hmm. A place to sit and pray in front of that grave. Interesting. Haven't seen that before." And then that voice again, "Yes. A place to sit and pray." And I go, "Oh! Ok." So I start to walk towards the bench and I see a ray of light come out of the clouds and illuminate the resting place in front of it, (I have the picture to prove it!) and I look more closely at that resting place.

My eyes go wide with complete wonder and I have trouble believing what I'm seeing. As I get closer I can see, it's true! There is a sculpture of an eagle feather headdress-wearing, peace pipe-carrying Native American Chief on that resting place! And my heart is bursting in my chest and I'm like "Who IS that?! I must know whose resting place that is!" and I walk up mesmerised by this Chief, with tears streaming down my face and I read the headstone and it says, "Here lies HERENA TARETARE PANAPA Beloved wife of the late Bill Panapa, loving mother of Penny and Vaughan and loved Nan to all her *mokos* (grandchildren)..." and next to that is a plaque saying,

"Blessed by the Lord for her healing hands." This was Vaughan's mother! This was the exact spot, where, twelve months earlier, I had prostrated!

And I sat on the bench opposite the Chief and Herena and I wept and wept.

After I prayed there I went home and bought tickets to return in TWO days! - to a home I hadn't seen in 23 years.

> *Call to me and I will answer you and show you great and hidden things that you have not known.*
>
> -Jeremiah 33:3

Chapter 8

Journey to Turtle Island[1]

Shortly after I bought the tickets to Denver I called my brother, Craig, and said, "Ok bro! I've bought the tickets and I get into Denver in two days! Let's meet up at the airport and rent a car and then drive up to the Rez (Wind River Indian Reservation, where we used to live with our father). We can visit Lyle (a Shoshoni medicine man and my father's best friend) and it will be like visiting Dad." (Our father passed away in November 2007). Just before I hung up Craig said, "Wait! I just remembered that a couple of years ago I had a dream about this! You called me and we decided to

---

1   "Turtle Island" is a term that some Native Americans use when referring to North America.

meet in Denver and we rented a brown car and we drove up to the Reservation together. When we got there you flew to the moon and discovered your true purpose and your true love! I got jealous and woke up." We both laughed and I thought: "Wow! This is going to be some trip!"

Craig and I had a great trip to the reservation together and we did meet up with Lyle and Marie Wadda. I remember my father speaking fondly about Lyle and telling me a story about him so I could appreciate that he walks in ways beyond my understanding. My father told me that Lyle does things like get a vision, drive all the way to California, go into a post office where a man is standing in line, stand next to that man and say a prayer and then return all the way back home to Wyoming. I thought that was amazing and it gave me a sense of admiration for Lyle although I had no idea how he does what he does. When I first met Lyle more than 20 years earlier he told me "I can't talk with you. You speak from your head, not your heart." And he got up and left the room. I was confused. My dad clearly loved this friend of his and had a deep respect for him but Lyle wouldn't even speak to me! At the time I did not understand. It was only years of experience that would teach me what he meant.

Another story we remembered was how when I was visiting Craig at his college, I was seated in the lobby waiting for him and someone came up from behind and put their hands over my eyes and said, "Surprise!" I turned around and the girl (Craig's girlfriend) who had put her hands over my eyes shrieked and said, "Oh my God! I thought you were Craig!" We definitely looked quite alike in those years of our youth.

I shared these memories with Craig as we drove through the primordial landscape of Wyoming. As we drove and reminisced, the skyline formed incredible patterns of powerful shapes with streaming rays of light moving across the landscape. Rain and light intermingled; black skies with columns of light moving across the landscape.

When we arrived on the reservation I noticed they had built a casino and also that my favourite place to eat, where my father used to take us, a small diner where they served Indian tacos, was no longer there. Both of those changes made me a little sad. Still, it was really, really good to be home.

We arrived at Lyle and Marie's home and it felt like no time had passed. The house looked the same to me and the landscape looked the same. Lyle and Marie came out to greet us with warmth and joy. That afternoon Lyle spoke with us more than he spoke with me in all our times together previously combined. I think he must have felt happy to see his good friend's sons and it was like visiting our father through us too. Lyle showed us a great deal of kindness that day. Some of the other family members came over, like his son who took me for walks through the mountains when I was a youth. We spoke about those memories and they asked me about my life during the past two decades away from Wyoming. Lyle's daughter-in-law is a healer and she showed us some traditional medicine she had with her and gifted it to us.

Lyle shared a number of stories about my father and my heart ached with gratitude and a deep missing of his humble nobility. That day Lyle shared a story with Craig and me that clarified a mystery about my father which I share in chapter 10, My Father's Wisdom.

My dear brother Craig had bought some fireworks on the drive up to the reservation and he took delight in sharing those with the children and family that had come to see us. It was a good way to end the day.

Craig and I drove back down to Denver airport and he flew back to San Francisco. I stayed at the airport waiting for two people who had flown in from Alaska who were due to land within a couple of hours of Craig's departure.

The two people I was to meet were sundancers on their way to dance in the Black Hills of South Dakota and they were going to rent a car and drive from Denver to Hill City, South Dakota.

So several hours after my brother flew back home from that same airport, I met them in the baggage claim area. It was a good meeting. One was from the Tsimshian tribe and one was Mohawk and both had been sundancers with the Lakota in the Black Hills for some years now. I didn't know much about the sundance ceremony. I thought perhaps I was being invited so that I could offer prayers from the side so that I could support their dance in that way. We drove off together towards the East sharing lots of good stories and laughter.

As we neared the Black Hills the others began to look for sage along the side of the road and we would occasionally stop to see if there was good sage to pick for the ceremony. They taught me how to do this and I felt very grateful to them. We stopped a few times until the last time when there was a place with hills on the side of the road and an abundance of sage. As I gathered I meditated on what they taught me: *to sprinkle some tobacco in asking permission of the plant, in gratitude and acknowledging one of our family members. Not to pick the mother plant (the tallest of the plants in each cluster) and not to pick all of the remaining plants in the group, so that the sage can continue to proliferate.*

I prayed while I picked the sage. At one point I looked up the hill and saw a steep but accessible place where a group of sage plants grew. I decided that would be the last group of sage I would pick from today. I walked towards that cluster and paused at another family of sage and picked a few from there. A strong thought and emotion hit me as I prayed. "Why are you only praying for the medicine now? This was your own PhD to protect them and if you don't pray for them who will? Why do you not include prayers for your plant family when you pray each day?" I felt humbled and vowed to include prayers for the plants each day. I then climbed the last slippery steps on the shale hillside to the cluster of sage I had decided to be the last pick for the day. As I reached down, acknowledging the mother plant the sunlight illuminated a beautiful crystal next to the plant. My heart swelled in my chest and I felt the gratitude reciprocated from the mother of the sage for this gift.

We arrived in the Black Hills and we drove to meet Ben Rhodd the Sundance Chief. He was watching and encouraging his son who was playing in a baseball game in the field. I watched the two sundancers go up to Ben and greet him. I don't actually recall if we spoke then although I'm pretty sure we were introduced and that it was fairly simple with few words exchanged. I do remember very clearly that as I turned to walk back to the car a light rain began and I felt a sense of not knowing why I was there and questioning whether my being there would be meaningful for anyone or of any use. I felt that emotion swell with each step over the grass to an almost desperate cry of prayer from my heart, "Let me serve in a good way!" As I said that prayer my eyes filled with tears of feeling of insufficient mingled with yearning for celestial aid, and a beautiful triple rainbow formed and my tears turned to laughter.

After that, when we got to the place in the heart of the Black Hills where they would do sundance, some things happened that are perhaps too sacred to describe and I was given a peace pipe and invited to do *Hamblecha* (a vision quest) which involves fasting and praying for four nights and days. As I sat on the ground on the hill and prayed, I watched the sun set on the first night. I thought it would get darker; however as the sunlight faded in the hills, another bright light began to rise. I could see two clouds in the shape of wings of exactly the same shape with a space between them. The sky became brighter and brighter until the crest of the most impossibly large full moon rose above the hills. It filled the space between the two wings and then as it continued to rise, one wing went west and another wing went east. I was stunned by the brilliance of this seemingly impossibly large full moon. As this occurred I remembered my brother's dream that I would fly to the moon on this trip and discover my true purpose and my true love.

After the vision quest I was walking with the Sundance Chief. We were walking and we got to a certain spot and he stopped and pointed to the ground and said that something happened here a long time ago. "There was a man standing where you're standing. He was a painter and he loved to paint. He had a wife and a young child and wanted to be able to support his family, so he was looking for work as an artistic painter. He saw that there was an advertisement in the paper for a job at Haskell Indian Nations University as a painter there. He was very happy about this so he contacted them and was accepted into the job.

When he started the job he found out that this wasn't the kind of painting that he expected. He wasn't doing artistic painting. He was painting these walls white. So there was all these hallways in the buildings of the school and he was just painting them white. It was really hard. It was like soul crushing to have his creativity and spiritual impulse denied and to just be painting these walls white. So he got sadder and sadder, and eventually he felt like he couldn't do this any more. This was something that was violating his spirit. So he walked away from that job. He went for a long journey or a 'walkabout', as the Aboriginal people in Australia would say.

He came back to this land, to where we are standing now. He was praying to Grandfather, to the Creator, and crying out and saying, 'What's happening! I want to support my family but my spirit is ill from this kind of painting. I want to praise the Creator with my gifts.' He reaches down and there is a piece of leather sticking out of the ground and he grabs this piece of leather. And while he's talking to the Creator and crying, tears tracing down his face, he starts to play with this piece of leather. He doesn't even notice what he is doing, he is so caught up in his prayer. By the time he has finished his prayer, he looks down at his hands. Now this piece of leather, he didn't know it, but this was his own grandfather's bridle from his horse from a long time ago. While he was praying he had been creating a piece of leather-work. Without even knowing, he had a little knife in his hand and he didn't know what his hands were doing until he looked down after the prayer and saw this incredible piece of art. While he was praying, he had been blessed, and had become a master leather worker. He spent the rest of his life practising that. He had found his purpose, but not in the way he had expected and put all his energy into prior to that prayer."

Chapter 9

Nudges from Grandfather

I saw and heard many other things on my vision quest that will remain private. I wasn't sure yet about my true purpose, but it was beginning to pull at me like some increasing sense of gravity.

After the vision quest finished I was unexpectedly invited to become a sundancer. On the morning of the third day of sundance the Sundance Chief was explaining the origins of sundance to everyone. He was explaining how a long time ago during a time of abundance the people began to take for granted the gifts of all their relations in nature. The people began to kill more than they needed and forgot to practise gratitude and reciprocity with mother earth in a good way. A famine swept the land because of this. During this time a prophet was given a vision of the ceremony of sundance to restore the balance. To restore the balance with humility and sacrifice there was nothing the people could offer that they hadn't been given… other than themselves. So sundance enables us to practise humility in our prayers of gratitude and giving back through the sacrifice of our own flesh. We pray and fast without food or water for four days and on the third day is the piercing where we sacrifice a piece of our own flesh for the earth.

Now this was on the third day of the sundance and I had heard about this "piercing". I had been told that it wasn't mandatory and that I could sundance without piercing. I have to admit when I thought about the idea of piercing I worried that maybe I did not know what my limits would be and whether I could do such a thing with honour and not fall prey to my own fears.

However on that third day when the sundance chief was explaining the origins of sundance as a way for humans to restore balance with the earth through humility and sacrifice, I felt a "pinch" on my right arm when he said the word "sacrifice". I looked to my right expecting to see someone but the nearest person was a distance away from me. I then thought, "That was a very real pinch. Who did that?"

Suddenly I felt my grandfather Borrah next to me and I realised he was asking me to pierce. From that point on I felt no fear and was confident in knowing I was meant to offer myself in this way, which I did.

Four days after sundance finished we went to the top of the mountain, *Hinhan Kaga*[1] and did a peace pipe ceremony facing the four directions and prayed for humanity. Privately I also said a prayer that if there is someone out there who can walk in this path of service to spirit and would be ok with being apart at times because of such demands of spirit, if such a woman was out there … I think I'm ready to meet her.

When I came off of Hinhan Kaga I checked my email for the first time in weeks. The first message in my inbox was from someone I had not met before. Her name was Lisa Michelle Silvers. She wrote that she had seen some posts I had written on a Native American Baháʼí Facebook page and understood from my posts that I was coming to Vancouver Island area to visit my mother. Lisa noticed that my mother lived on the island beside her, and I would probably travel through if I was going to take the ferry that connected to my mother's home. Lisa wondered if we could meet and discuss our experiences in Indian country; to convey some of the correct

---

1   Lakota Sioux for "Making of Owls". Colonist history gave a different name of "Harney Peak".

protocols for distinctive groups, share how Indigenous Knowledge holders had influenced our world view and how that impacted our life and work. I looked for her profile on Facebook and saw a picture of the comedienne Carol Burnett as Nora Desmond, a silent film actress in a take-off of Sunset Boulevard. Lisa had no 'selfies' and so I just wasn't sure who she was in any of the photos. I saw someone who had sunglasses and a white streak in her hair with a bunch of children and thought she was possibly a mature aged mother of many children.

After I wrote to Lisa to say that I would try to stop by on my way, I called my mother to reconfirm that I would be arriving in several days' time. She explained that something had happened with her husband such that I wouldn't be able to visit the way I had originally hoped. It might be a few weeks before I could. I had no idea what to do with myself to wait for several weeks. That sense of loss and slight panic turned into a blessing when the Sundance Chief, Ben Rhodd invited me to hang out with him in the meanwhile. That meant I got to sit on the balcony with Ben at sunsets and listen to his stories into the nights.

When my mom let me know that she was ready, I said a grateful goodbye to Ben. As I left he described something called "The Gathering of Eagles," an inter-tribal spiritual unity gathering, happening later in the month if I was free to return. I made a mental note, then wrote to Lisa to apologise for my delay and silence. If she was available could we still visit when I changed ferries in Victoria? Lisa teased me mischievously; said she figured I had changed my mind since she was some strange anonymous woman. It turns out she was able to meet with me on the day I was coming. When I saw her, my first thought was "She's not old at all!" In contrast to the ostentatious, crazed look of the character on her profile picture, Lisa glowed with a playful and youthful energy. She had freedom of spirit. We ended up taking food together, talking and walking along the Dallas Road waterfront trail for several hours.

Of the many things we discussed, one which stands out in my memory is the impact that Dr Peter Khan had had in each of our lives. Dr Khan, who had served as a member of the Universal House of Justice, radiated a logical adherence to spiritual reality and together with his wife, Dr Janet Khan, made a consistent effort in the advancement of women. We discovered that Drs Khan had engendered in each of us a devotion to striving to understand, and to engage in true scholarship. I became so excited that I spontaneously related to Lisa a pivotal meeting with Dr Peter Khan. When I was a twenty-year-old volunteer security guard in Israel at the Bahá'í World Centre, I had asked the Bahá'í Research Department if there were any letters from the beloved Guardian of the Bahá'í

Faith, Shoghi Effendi, written to my grandfather. I was surprised and a little nervous to be called into Dr Khan's office. He, on behalf of the Universal House of Justice had for me some letters written by the Guardian to my family. Dr Khan described correspondence to my grandfather as largely administrative and financial in nature, documents, requests to acquire properties on behalf of the Faith and the like.

Dr Khan went on to say, "However, we did feel that you would be very interested in these three letters from the Guardian to your grandmother Martha Louise Kavelin." He proceeded to show me copies of letters written both by the Guardian's secretary and the Guardian himself during the 1940s, including one letter written prior to my grandfather becoming a Bahá'í. It acknowledged my grandmother's request for the Guardian's prayers that my grandfather might also fall in love with the Bahá'í Faith. At the bottom, the Guardian had included in his own handwriting, a supplication in honour of my grandfather.

The second letter was written in response to my grandmother's news that my mother, the eldest, had been born. This too included a prayer in the Guardian's hand. The third letter was to celebrate the occasion of the birth of my twin uncles. I have remained grateful to him because I had the further privilege of sending the prayer for my mother, to my mother.

Lisa and I walked and walked and spoke candidly about many things, much of it around our attempts and sometimes comic failings at purity and service; and our yearning to make concerted and continual efforts to develop in the practical application of spiritual reality. I felt she had a great sense of humour, fierce empathy, illuminating intuition and refreshing honesty; I saw in her a genuine compassion for those with challenges in life, a love for children, animals, plant-life, bird-life. She had an independent spirit, purity of heart and a keen intellect, which she tried to use to correlate significant spiritual principles with the needs and thoughts of society.

Towards the end of our walking together the sun had set and we faced the ocean as we were saying goodbye. Lisa asked that we say a prayer together. We sat on a bench facing the Pacific Ocean and Lisa sang a prayer. Her beautiful voice caught me by surprise. I felt that I wanted to also sing a prayer and I stood and sang the prayer I used to sing with my daughter *O God Guide Me*. While I was singing that a light grew in the horizon and the full moon rose out of the ocean. As the last note of the prayer finished and I looked at the moon I remembered my brother's dream had two parts to it. "True purpose and true love". I looked at Lisa and then back to the moon and then back to Lisa again with a sense of awe, wonder and curiosity.

I took the ferry to see my mom and on that day two things happened. I discovered the news that while Lisa and I had been walking and talking, Dr Peter Khan had passed away. It hit both Lisa and me quite hard and established a unique connection of feeling that grief and loss for a loved one.

The next thing that happened was that as I sat with my mother in her office overlooking the beautiful islands between Salt Spring Island and Vancouver Island she said, "I found that picture of your grandfather that you love." I had lost it from my old computer having been emailed a copy the year before. So my mother emailed me the photo of my grandfather across the room as it were. In that photo my grandfather isn't posed and he is laughing with some Native American friends in the midst of people with food in their hands. I love how natural he looks. I didn't know he had any connections with Native Americans until I saw that photo.

I decided that I would put that photo on the Native American Bahá'í Facebook page to ask if anyone knew who the people laughing with my grandfather are so I could see if they are still alive and ask them to share stories about my grandfather. So I posted the photo on Facebook and turned in my chair to let my mother know when I had done it. In the time it took to tell her, someone had already posted a reply. It was Lisa! She wrote, "I was at the home of Ted and Joan Anderson in Red Deer Alberta, four years ago, scanning and digitizing a lot of Joan's photos to preserve them for archives, and hanging out with Ted senior. Joan recorded EVERY-THING. She was awesome like that. I found that photo in one of her albums. I got an email address for your uncle John through official channels. I think I sent it to your mother at the same time, or your uncle forwarded it to her. I can get you the names of the people in the photo with your grandad."

I felt my grandfather nudge me again. This time he smiled and winked.

That photo provides the front cover of this book.

Chapter 10

My Father's Wisdom

Honouring my father Dr Bruce Jones this morning I remembered when I was a child we had a station wagon with quite a bit of rust on it. When I was about five I remember seeing a Porsche drive past us and I said, "Wouldn't it be great if we could afford to buy a Porsche!" My father said, "We can afford to." I said, "Then why don't we get a Porsche?!" He said, "We don't need one." That simple statement stayed with me the rest of my life.

When I was about seventeen-years-old I started to go to the gym and was focused on having a nice body. I bought a second hand convertible car and being attractive to the opposite sex became a focus for me. During that year while we were driving my father expressed his concern to me. *"Be careful who you pretend to be. You will attract a woman who is interested in what you are pretending to be rather than in you. If you want to attract your soul mate, then become your true spiritual self. Wherever she is in the world she will be attracted to you and you will then be able to find each other."*

Later in life my father passed away with relatively little financially even though at times he had held high-paying jobs such being the director of a large psychiatric unit in a big hospital. He was extremely humble and did not talk with me about his philanthropy. I learned from others that he did things like buying an abandoned high school in an urban black area and transformed it into a youth centre. That he developed relationships with, and encouraged celebrities to work with disadvantaged youth in making theatre productions; that he bought a mobile home which he filled with computers and took to reservations to train Native American youth in computer literacy skills.

We lived on the Wind River Indian Reservation for some time. There we were on the first Bahá'í Local Spiritual Assembly together, the rest of the members were Shoshoni and Arapahoe tribal members. When beloved Universal House of Justice member Mr Hushmand Fatheazam heard of this he asked me if I would ask my father to write a book about how that historic first Assembly formed. I just said, "I don't think my father would feel comfortable talking about himself like that." I did ask.

When my father passed away my step-mother Nina Jones wrote that in all their years of marriage she never once heard him say anything bad about anyone. Ever. It was a shock to read that because I realised it was absolutely true. I took that for granted. The reason I never noticed was because it was just natural to his character. He never spoke negatively about anyone in his entire life. I've never met anyone else with that quality. The day before he passed away, my Dad told me how proud he was of me and of the PhD I had just finished. During the hour I was making my oral defence to the law faculty on *honouring and protecting Indigenous knowledge*, my father passed away. Having had him express his approval and encouragement has remained an abiding source of strength and steadfastness for me.

My father treasured living on the Wind River Indian Reservation and in the years he lived there he fell in love with the mountains and the people. I always felt sad when I thought about how he left the reservation and that he seemed very sad about leaving. I never understood why. Years later in 2011 my brother and I travelled back to the reservation to visit my father's best friend, Lyle, who is a medicine man. Lyle shared a story that explained so much. He said that my father had discovered a systemic injustice in the government health system on the reservation and that it was having a negative impact on the people of the reservation. When he discovered this he knew that if he reported it that his life would change. He went for a long walk in the mountains and prayed. When he returned he chose to report the injustice of the health system to the authorities. They couldn't fire him but they moved him off the reservation and he suffered in that loss. He moved his job to Haskell Indian Nations University, but I could see that sadness linger. I knew that broke his heart but he never said anything to me about it. Hearing this now from Lyle gave me an understanding of my father's commitment to justice and the silent sacrifice for the people, which characterised much of his actions.

About two years after my father's passing I was saying a prayer for the departed for him:

> *O my God! O Thou forgiver of sins, bestower of gifts, dispeller of afflictions!*
>
> *Verily, I beseech thee to forgive the sins of such as have abandoned the physical garment and have ascended to*

the spiritual world.

O my Lord! Purify them from trespasses, dispel their sorrows, and change their darkness into light. Cause them to enter the garden of happiness, cleanse them with the most pure water, and grant them to behold Thy splendors on the loftiest mount.

- 'Abdu'l-Bahá

After I finished the prayer I had a profound moment where I heard my father's voice. Normally when I have possible guidance from the spiritual realm it comes as a creative thought and not a literal voice. On this occasion I could hear the actual timbre of my father's voice. He said, "Thank you for praying for my forgiveness. I want you to know that when you pray for my forgiveness that you are also praying for yourself and your children. Because my sins of omission or commission are then transformed in your life and in the lives of your children, into blessings."

I'm so grateful for his guidance and continued presence in my life.

Chapter 11

Three Visits from Her

When I was five years old I first met her in a dream.

In that dream I was standing at the bottom of a hill. On top of that hill was an old-style stone wall. On top of that wall was a girl about twelve. Her eyes were filled with unconditional love, compassion and exquisite kindness. I felt completely loved and fulfilled. It was a brief but powerful dream. When I awoke I felt a pang of loss. Where did she go? I looked under my bed and then in the wardrobe and went outside into the garden to look behind the bushes. I looked for her for a long time. Over the following years I always kept my eye out for her. When I was twelve I had a conversation with my mother, "It says in the Bahá'í Writings that the minimum age for marriage is fifteen-years-old. If I find her when I'm fifteen can I marry her?" My mother must have felt that was a safe bet and agreed.

In 1987 I had just turned nineteen and was serving in the Holy Land at the Bahá'í World Centre as a youth volunteer. Soon after my arrival I had another profound dream. I was flying in front of the Shrine of Bahá'u'lláh (the Prophet-Founder of the Bahá'í Faith.) There was a pathway of white stones lined with cypress trees and I was flying at the height of those trees. I was using my hands to flap, however I couldn't seem to fly higher than the tops of those trees. There were three men below me who looked like Mafia characters and they had shotguns. They were shooting at me. I would push harder, flapping with one hand, and glide slowly to one side and just miss being shot. Then I would push harder with the other moving to the other side. This continued and I felt fear.

Suddenly out of the clouds above, a woman with beautiful large white wings emerged. She soared with power and grace towards me. When she came up to me she unfolded the same white wings from my own back. I had thought I was using my hands to fly, but I hadn't realised I was using the tips of my wings not yet unfolded.

Three Visits from Her

Now with my wings unfolded, they burst open with joy, freedom and power and we soared off together; the danger of the three men evaporated as if a mirage. We soared through the clouds together in a dance of weaving flight and then dove into an ancient forest of huge trees and untouched beauty. We splashed each other as we soared over soft, green moss-banked streams and through waterfalls and resulting rainbows.

I awoke from that dream and felt that same feeling as when I was five. I wondered if perhaps if this dream figure was a real-life person I had just met the week before. I recall having a conversation with a mentor of mine, the great poet Roger White, telling him about the dream and my musings on her identity although I don't recall how he responded.

In June 2004 I had another dream. This time I saw the most beautiful love poem I've ever seen and it was engraved in pure light on tablets of chrysolite, a substance like translucent diamonds. I woke from this dream and the poem was still with me! I was so happy that I could remember it. Content, I drifted off back to sleep; then awoke again with a start. The memory of the words of that exquisite poem had disappeared. Unable to go back to sleep I went to my study and began to say prayers. Suddenly I felt something forming like a cloud in the air to my left. I froze in surprise and did not turn my head to look directly. This cloud coalesced and became the poem from my dream, but this time I was awake! The poem stayed briefly in that form and then it began to coalesce further until there, robed in white, was a beautiful woman who radiated a great warmth of compassion, unconditional love and gentle kindness.

I did not turn to look at her directly but I broke my stasis and asked earnestly, "Who are you?" She replied, "Do you not recognise me?" Again I asked, "Who are you?" She then said softly "You met me and searched for me as a child and again as a youth. Now I visit you as an adult." For a third time I asked, "Who are you?" She paused and looked within as if asking permission to see if I was ready to hear it. Then with gentle nobility she replied, "I am your soul and a face of God." I was in a state of total awe and wonder.

She then said, "I must leave you again, for I have to return to the Abha Kingdom" (the spiritual realm). I protested, "How can I bear this separation? I will weep and burn!" She said, "Take comfort that I return to dance in flight; you are being recreated in this dance and being given new gifts. If you cannot bear the separation, turn towards the Holy Threshold and sometimes you may see me prostrate there."

Everything changed in that moment. My self-understanding, my understanding of the true spiritual self of other humans, no matter what stage of development they are at … the way I understood the possibilities of love between God and humanity, between humans and with everything in the world changed in that moment.

In the morning I began to doubt myself. "You're going through a difficult time in life. Perhaps your subconscious created this vision so that you would feel better." In the midst of the doubt I suddenly had a strong thought, "Go to the closet in your bedroom. On the top shelf is a briefcase. In there is a letter waiting for you." I immediately went to the wardrobe and found the briefcase. I hadn't opened it in more than ten years. It was full of correspondence from my time in the Holy Land. I carefully went through each letter and reminisced, however I couldn't find anything that addressed my current state of doubt. Then at the bottom of the pile of letters was an envelope. It was unopened. In elegant handwriting it simply said "From Roger to Chris." It was a letter from Roger White.

I carefully opened the letter and began to read, filled with wonder, gratitude and certitude. "Chris, I feel it is endearing that you felt that the winged woman in your dream might be the person you just met. It shows your openness and trust in others. However from everything I have read in the writings and from my own understanding of dreams, this woman was your soul."

My heart burst with gratitude and overflowed down my cheeks.

Some days later as I drove my children to school I had a vision that further comforted me with certitude and I pulled over asking for one of my children for a crayon so that I could write down what I saw.

My Magnum Opus

Through our symphony of propinquity,
We are opened to hear every lament of anguish in the world;
yet we are also opened to hear Her answering Call,
of the healing songs of light and love.

A harmony of Her Love resonates through the universe,
A foundational note vibrates through the core.
Loving kinship unlocks the secret hearing of it.
A silent, singing note calls to our hearts,
Its ambrosial jasmine fragrance familiar, its celestial origins clear,
Like the embrace of a long-lost beloved,
we open ourselves to dilation and follow the threading light of its celebration,
through to the gossamer thin veil of unending depth,
where countless motes of light weave their dance of resurrection/recreation,
singing and shining the infinite spectrum of myriad Names of Her.

I dilate in the silent communion with you in prayer and service

Three Visits from Her

*and make myself expand
until I touch the fringes of our own dance
of propinquity and luminescence,
brushing softly against some feathered movement of meaning,
to soar to that place where the essence of music lives,
that unending, unfolding opus magnum, being written in the space between us,
where our utterly unique shining beauty intimately intertwines,
a miracle,
coalescing into a celebration that dances a new name of Her,
that sings a song, heard nowhere else, and now everywhere,
giving pause to all of creation so that all may now celebrate this new song.*

*Unable to sustain such flight forever,
I fall back into this world,
waking to see that only the single silent note sings softly in my heart.
I still hear the cries of suffering and separation,
yet I have also heard the answer of our symphony.
How can I be away from this soul embrace of kinship-love and celebration?
How may I return?
The veil is too dense and too remote, the distance so great!*

*I weep in separation, I have returned,
but have left my heart and soul behind with you!
I gather myself together.
I seek to make a lasso of my will,
Throwing it, tying it to the worlds,
My feet firmly planted,*

Every fibre of my being straining to draw together the two worlds,
So that the song may be heard by all.
But it is too much! My strength cannot match the infinity of the distance,
Or the density of the veil.
I lament my inadequacy
And cry in grief.

I hear a voice gently call to me,
"Do not suffer so! The separation is not what it appears!
Now hear My loving secret of comfort:
The distance is not great between worlds,
Its span is within the space between the walls of your heart!
The veil is yourself!
Therefore burn in service to Me!
Burn the veil of self!
By this the worlds you long to unite,
will embrace as one,
and I will step down from My throne on high,
and live in the hearts of all,
So that this earth becomes the paradise of love.

Thus you will be reunited with Her
and the worlds will merge,
and your feathered dance of light with each other
will no longer be hidden,
but shine resplendent
everywhere, in everyone."

Thus my friend, we will love each other in this dance of propinquity,

Three Visits from Her

Unfolding our symphony, inviting all to add the unique beauty
Of their celestial voices,
Merging to form a celebration of such diverse beauty,
That it attracts Her very Soul,
Whereupon she will Sing the Song of Her Love,
throbbing throughout the universe and now heard by all,
Singing in all our hearts and we will finally be at peace.
No more cries of anguish heard,
But only,
Love! Love! Love!

Conclusion

There is no past – everything is still happening.

- Uncle Banjo Clarke

These stories are not objects of consumption or voyeurism; they are invitations to you into active, sacred relationships of service to others and 'with others'.

"Writing" this "conclusion" was nearly impossible for all kinds of reasons. It took me a while to give myself permission to write it. There were dangers lurking I couldn't put my finger on.

The best way to kill a story is to write it down.

The kind of stories I've told in this book may seem 'miraculous' to some, yet are actually common in the Indigenous world where such stories are kept alive through the continuity of a living oral tradition. There is hesitancy among many Elders to write down the oral traditions that contain many stories like the ones I have shared in this book. This is not a challenge of literacy or discomfort with 'writing'. It has more to do with their knowledge of the risk to you, the reader, of assuming the story is now 'complete' in its written form. It risks these sacred stories becoming fixed, inert, concretised. Dead.

Such stories are not the closed circles one might assume when closing the book's cover. These stories don't live within the two-dimensional perspective of the flat page. If you follow the promptings of your heart and rise higher, your vision shifts and you realise that these circles are actually open ended. Infinitely unfolding spirals. The reality is that when sharing such stories the listener is invited into those relationships. In English there is no aorist past tense continuing to convey that something that happened in the past is still happening now, or that what is happening now is happening in the future. This narrative aorist tense is present in Ancient Greek and is a hallmark of the Aboriginal concept of the '*Dreamtime.*'

By the very act of witnessing these stories through reading this book or listening to it read aloud ... you have been invited into dialogue with your own ancestors and the ancestors of those in the stories. You yourself become the living location of that dialogue between ancestors in the next world. The real question now is: how does that dialogue call you into prayerful action in service to others now?

If you have feelings of insufficiency in contemplating such a step, "I don't know how to do that," it's okay to have those thoughts; and in a way that's a good step of humility, to acknowledge our dependency upon the spiritual realm. Because in the end, it's not just about you, or about me alone and unaided. It's about a mutually reinforcing relationship with the hundreds and thousands of generations of your own ancestors standing, soaring behind you, waiting to move through your will; healing old wounds within you, healing wounds between peoples. *Those in the next world patiently wait for us to pray for them as they pray for us. In such prayerful connection there is a mingling of condition and a mingling of station. In such a mingling there is call to action. Those in the next world rely upon us so they can act through us; when we arise in service to others we are given new gifts of capacity we didn't dream we could possess.*

There is a case to suggest this is mirrored in our genetics. About ten years ago I read an article about a Western scientific discovery (a discovery long known to many Indigenous knowledge holders.) Scientists observed that honeybees have latent genes which are only unlocked when the bees perform certain actions, like a particular bee dance with other bees. Suddenly the bee has a new capacity unlocked. Is it so difficult to imagine that each of us has many, many latent capacities that are activated *only* when we perform the actions where those particular capacities are required? In actions involving service to others, where we must necessarily go outside what is comfortable or familiar?

It can be a deep blessing to discover or remember that we are loved and not alone.

This morning while writing this conclusion I remembered a day about six years ago when I was in Rarotonga at the home of a beautiful Elder of the Pacific, Aunty Paddy. Her full name is Eleitino Edwina Diana Patricia Walker. She was maybe ninety-two years old at the time and actively involved in transforming education for children and in making musical albums and books for children. I remember walking into her stunning home. It was completely white. She had a door with a carved white swan on it. Everything in the home was varying shades of white. Everything. She told me she didn't get a TV until she found one that was white.

Conclusion

We went to her table in the back yard overlooking the beautiful blue ocean. She shared with me that she was concerned she might be passing soon and that she felt she had work still to complete and didn't want to leave yet. While we were speaking she looked past me, like she was looking at the other side of the yard and said, "Oh there they are." I paused and asked "Who?" she said, "My grandmother." We then talked a little about the next world and I tried to comfort her sense of anxiousness. Later that night I woke at about 3am inspired with a letter for Aunty Paddy. The next day she accepted the letter and ambled into the back garden as she read to herself; she stopped walking at the point where the edge of her garden meets the ocean sands. When finished, she returned with tears in her eyes; Aunty Paddy said she cherished the letter and would read it each day the rest of her life.

Recalling that time, I wrote to a friend to ask if Aunty Paddy (Eleitino Pia) was still alive because I wanted to ask her permission to reprint the letter I wrote her. She would have been about ninety-eight now. After I sent the email, I found out that she had actually passed away last July, 2015. Hopeful of her blessing to share, these were the contents of my letter,

"Dearest Eleitino Pia,

I won't ever forget the joy of meeting you. You have imprinted my soul with your noble grace, ethereal beauty, and youthful enthusiasm, compassionate spirit of service to humanity, wonderful humour, love of children, and the music that sings from your heart.

I remember your concern about leaving unfinished business behind and your transition to the next world. I have felt a longing to comfort you and so I have woken after only several hours of sleep, in the spiritual hours before dawn to write to you and offer you this gift. I wish to briefly explore with you with childlike wonder what the next world will be like for you and the joy of that journey of adventure.

I wish you peace and contentment.

I want to share with you some of the things I know about the souls of the next world and how they work with us here.

You know children very well. When you first teach a child something complex like building a pyramid made of blocks you gently and lovingly show them how it is done, cradling their hands in your own, moving the blocks slowly and letting their hands feel the movement and weight of the blocks. At first the child does not understand what is happening, but towards the end when the very last block is placed on top of the pyramid they see the pattern and understand the movement of their hand in your own and see what has been accomplished. They then raise their chubby little arms in the air in victory, shouting with gleeful pride as if to say, "Look what I accomplished!" looking into your eyes with self-delight. Their eyes boastfully proclaim that they could show you how if you like. You can only laugh with tender affection, proud that the child has owned what they have learned from you. You are more than happy for them to assume that they discovered how to build that pyramid themselves and that they built it all on their own.

But if that child turns to you at that last minute of realisation and looks into your eyes and says, "Thank you for having taught me. Thank you for having helped me. I love you." Our hearts expand in the most unusual way and we long to teach them more. And if that child not only shows gratitude to us but goes to other children and begins to teach them how sharing their gifts of learning can help them, our hearts are filled with love for them, wanting to shower them with all we know and help them achieve great things.

This is how the souls of the next world are with us (and how we can be with each other in this world.) We are the children and they inspire us with our greatest works in the world, happy for us to think we did it ourselves. And like us, they are also inspired to shower us with extra blessings when we express our humility and gratitude to them and use those blessings in service to others in sharing what we are given.

Paddy, the songs you have sung that have moved your heart most in the world, the works of love you have crafted, these have been inspired by ones who love you in the next world. Souls who deeply love you, like your grandmother. You have been nurtured by her and others all your life even when you did not see their footprints in the sand next to you.

You have given light to many people in this world, your virtues sing strong and true. If only an hour with you has changed my life with seeing the beauty of those virtues I cannot begin to imagine how many lives have been uplifted because of who you are. Just being who are you are shines that light. You don't need to DO anything. Just connect your heart to God and the unique spectrum of the light of your soul will sing a song in this universe heard nowhere else and all of creation will sing back in response this new song.

When you pass into the next world, which is within this world, you will only leave behind your physical limitations. Your body (however beautiful it may be) is only a sculpted work of art that the soul uses to express itself in this world. When you leave your body you will be liberated to express the full potential of your souls, and all the virtues you have acquired are the new beautiful spiritual body you will have through which you will move and sing and shine your purpose into the world. You will become the soul that cradles the tiny hands of others and inspires them to be who they truly are. You will cradle the hands of your daughter and sing her into being who she truly is.

You will be able to sing through the hearts of those of us who love you most. I fully expect you to inspire me as I sing and dance my service in the Islands of the Pacific. I will pray for you each day as I know you will pray for me from the other side of that thin veil that separates the ocean from the sky."

Each of us has those in the next world who love us and wish to assist us. These include our own ancestors who have passed on. Even if they didn't express love in this world in ways that were best, they have realisations in the next world of their mistakes and wish to make amends. There are also souls in the next world who might not be related to us, but they see the small moments of our efforts to help someone they love or they see us trying to do something that is important to their own hearts. They then 'adopt' us and begin to help us. There are also other layers of spiritual reality that I am learning more about, like Angels and other Holy Beings, who are more powerful. Then there is the Holy Spirit itself. The Divine

Energy or Grace of God that links all beings with great Compassion. The Holy Spirit is powerful, yet also intimate. We merely need to ask with faith, trust we will be answered, be determined in our efforts and continually act in service to others. Then those in the next world are able to help us with all of their gifts. "In prayer there is a mingling of condition. A mingling of station."[1]

I hope that you the reader have found meaningful insights in the stories within this book and the books to come in this series. My prayer is that each of you will grow in your paths of prayerful action in service to others and share courageously what you learn with others. I hope that I will hear your stories too and that I can also learn from your own growing realisations.

Not sure where to begin? That's a good sign, as it means you have the self-awareness that makes guidance from others in the next world possible to receive. The place to begin is with your heart. Are there injustices affecting others that move your heart? How can you transform yourself as part of efforts to bring restorative justice and to offer service to others? ASK for guidance and help from the spiritual realm through prayer. TRUST completely that you will be answered. Actively listen for an answer, whether it comes from a song, or a conversation, something in nature or a book. When the

---

[1] 'Abdu'l-Bahá', *'Abdu'l-Bahá' in London*, UK Bahá'í Publishing Trust, 1982, p96.

answer you are getting feels inspired to you, ACT. This action is the most important part of the process. If we are not engaged in action then we cannot be guided. It's okay to make mistakes. If your intentions are good and you are practising humility and are prayerfully reflective, those in the next world can use the momentum of your action to reorient your movement in the right direction. Be compassionate with yourself. It's okay that you have flawed thoughts and moments of selfishness or arrogance. My greatest moments of learning and guidance often followed a realisation that my thoughts were arrogant and then admitting to myself that a transformation of my thoughts was necessary. So, be steadfast and determined with complete trust that you will be guided. Repeat the process of asking for guidance and reflecting on your actions and on the emerging results at each phase so that you can refine both your movements and your awareness of the growing sets of relationships, (relationships both in this world and in the next) which are supporting the act of service. As you move on your path of service you will meet others whose hearts are also moved in such ways. People you are guided to. Consult with them as part of this process. You will find that teams begin to form around each act of service.

How does one apply the art of listening, to spirit? It begins with faith, which animates the listening itself. Expecting an answer when you ask a question. Even in normal human conversations if you don't expect answers to questions you would probably not be a very good listener! Perhaps the most crucial action in listening to spirit is to slow down. If you are rushing past the person you've asked a question of, your listening capacity is compromised.

A long, long time ago Buffalo White Calf Woman, a Lakota Prophet, was teaching her disciples. She told them that there would come a time when the world would begin to spin faster. People would selfishly try to turn the gifts that the Creator gave them into power for themselves. This would create shadows. People would try to consume these shadows; they would chase these illusions of their own power and consume them yet never feel full. As more and more people ran after these shadows, the world would spin faster. People would begin to say "We do not have enough time!" Parents would no longer have time for their children. Children would no longer respect their elders. The disciples listening to Buffalo White Calf Woman were dismayed by this story. They asked her, "what can we do when the earth begins to spin faster?" She replied, "the only thing you can do is to walk slower."

Materialism somehow seduces us into believing that if we run faster in our consumption, everything will be better. We will have better "things." While Spirit says, "Slow down. You have been given all you need. Open your eyes and see the gifts."

Epilogue

When We Tell Our Stories They Come Alive

Telling stories is a powerful Indigenous spiritual technology. It awakens relationships in both the spiritual realm and the physical realm. On one simple level, I like to think of those in the next world seeing us telling a story and then responding with, "she's ready! She's remembering us! Now's our chance to take it to the next stage!"

I was continually awe-struck while writing this book. Again and again relationships reawakened and important work was reignited. One of the main delays to finishing this book seemed to be that the act of recording the stories brought them to life and then activated the next stages of the story.

I actually noted some of these more recent developments within the chapters. There are a few more that I'll touch on here, briefly.

Contacting Camilla Chance for permission to reproduce the chapter, *Wisdom Man in Action,* led to her inadvertently sending me on a trip that allowed me to be with the Elder Clifford Cardinal again. Also, I met up with Christine Watson after ten years in order to ask permission to name her in this book and finally thank her for being instrumental in me meeting Lillian Holt. As it turns out, Christine is also a professional copy editor and she offered and acted as the copy editor for this book. More than this, we ended up doing work together while I wrote this book, organising workshops together on Spirituality and Social Transformation.

Several months ago, after I finished the book's first draft, I wanted to mail the relevant chapters to Ben Rhodd, my Sundance Chief; to follow protocol and to seek his permission to publish. Ben lived far away, on Turtle Island (United States). It would take some time for him to receive the books' contents. But for some reason, while each day I felt like I wanted to, something blocked me from sending it to him. It seemed like a simple act to take. But this went on for three

Epilogue

months and I didn't understand. Finally, after prayers again, I felt it was time. So at the end of January 2016, I wrote to ask Ben what was the best way to get him the chapters. An hour later he replied he thought it'd be better to email the chapters rather than by post because he was traveling. He was currently traveling around Australia and was in Melbourne. I live in Melbourne.

I wrote back to him to advise I was in Melbourne too and he said he was about to fly to Uluru; we could visit briefly on his return just before going back to Turtle Island. Then a couple of hours later, Juanita, who Ben is married to, emailed me to say that they missed their flight by minutes, and decided it must be a "Chris day." So Lisa Michelle, our dear friend Russell Tobin, and I were able to meet up with them, have dinner at the home of generous new friends and deliver the chapters to Ben personally. He gave consent to publish.

Two weeks ago I spent a day securing permission from various people to publish the chapter about William Cooper. I visited the German consulate and a Rabbi at the St. Kilda Synagogue. Then I had a meeting about a totally different matter with a brilliant woman named Maxine. We only had an hour to discuss something quite complex. But, I found myself compelled to share with her events that were totally off-topic, describing what I had been doing that morning with trying to honour this unsung hero, William Cooper.

I pulled out the chapter on William Cooper that I had in my bag; as I pushed it across the table said, "I know our meeting was supposed to be about something else, and we don't have much time, but I feel I needed to share this with you." She looked at the chapter for a while and then looked up at me and said, 'It's because my mother is William Cooper's blood niece and she was raised by him in his home."

There are many other examples like this, but I will have to wait until the next book to share because things are unfolding, which are sensitive, or in process and I need to wait before I can share those wonders with you.

kitamak kihyêw îniyew

Chris Kavelin

Medicine of Our Ancestors

Ancestors Are Medicine

The 2nd Book of the

Honouring Indigenous Spiritual Technologies Series

Chapter 1

Medicine Man

In February 2015 I was invited to speak in Edmonton, Canada at a conference called *Wisdom Engaged: Traditional Knowledge and Northern Community Well-Being*, held at University of Alberta Hospital. I was invited to give two presentations: a brief individual talk about traditional medicines and a keynote paper co-presented with John Hunter where we were speaking about a painting John had done. John comes from the Gamiliroy tribe, Northern New South Wales, Australia.

I have to admit that when I was on my way to this conference, I anticipated that it would be largely academic, with mostly Western researchers and possibly some minor Indigenous engagement. I was surprised to find that the reality was different from normal university-hosted conferences. It seemed the majority of participants were Indigenous and there was a significant number of senior Elders and traditional healers present. This surprised me because there is usually an uneasy alliance between universities and traditional healers. But this seemed to be a gathering that had stronger elements of community than academia.

In my first presentation I sang an opening prayer and then gave a brief talk on how the Western health system is very dependent on Indigenous medicines. In my talk I spoke about how my research showed that globally, the preponderance of all pharmaceutical drugs find significant origins from Indigenous peoples. This includes the majority of cancer drugs and HIV medicines.

During the period of colonisation when Europeans came to Africa, North America and other lands, the colonists had their own plant-based medicines useful for treating diseases and toxins. When they arrived they found there were entirely different diseases, which they were not familiar with. When they became sick, local healers would heal them and often share their knowledge with their guests. In spite of the problems of colonisation, there was a degree of sharing healing knowledge and there were no commercialisation issues. Additionally, maintaining a supply of medicines from Europe was a major issue because the time it took for ships to provide replacement supplies were usually prolonged and if a ship carrying medicines did not make it; that meant there would be no medicines for a long time. But local healers showed colonists alternative medicines for European illnesses. These alternative medicines became adopted as more sustainable and easily accessible in the new location. This is reflected in the first pharmacopoeias, or lists of national medicines in each country, where the bulk of medicines are listed as originating from Indigenous peoples. Then in the late 1800s the pharmacopoeia stopped acknowledging the origins of medicine from Indigenous peoples. Now we live in a time when the majority of medicines we are given actually originated from Indigenous peoples but the general population has no idea of this. What happened?

This sharing of medicines did not change until the late 1800s when two things happened. In Germany industrial chemists developed the capacity to make chemical compounds in factories and to synthesize organic plant compounds into pills. This was accompanied by the beginnings of patent laws designed to enable monopolies by companies who saw the opportunity to capitalise on the commercialisation of medicines. From this period on there was a gradual and intentional de-identification of both the plants and the

Indigenous peoples as the origins of medicines so that the exclusive ownership by corporations through patents could be justified.

In modern times this pattern of appropriation and de-identification has continued and nearly every major university in the Western world has programs of research developing medicines from Indigenous knowledge. However, the chain of research from postgraduate student to uptake by medium-size biotech companies, and finally to multinational pharmaceutical companies, usually de-identifies the origins of the active constituents of the medicines. Thus, the person taking modern medicines has no idea that her breast cancer medicine came from the bark of the Pacific Yew Tree or that it was taken from the knowledge of Native American tribes on the Pacific West coast.

What this means is that our current generations have a diminished capacity for expressing gratitude to Indigenous communities, their knowledge of local plants and to the plants themselves. We still have the capacity for gratitude. But we now have to do a lot of independent investigation to find out the true origins of the healing we may experience.

In the next section of my presentation I talked about having discovered that a number of HIV medicines have come from Indigenous communities.

After my presentation I went outside the lecture theatre and over to the refreshment table to make a coffee. A Native American Elder whom I had noticed earlier came up to me while I was making it. I had noticed earlier that he didn't talk much. My impression was that he was a man who had made great sacrifices for humanity along with great humility and integrity. When I first saw him I had a sense of my ancestors asking me to be obedient to him. He came over to me and said, "I enjoyed your talk. I got a lot out of it. We should talk further." We didn't talk much more than that, however his few words meant a great deal to me. His name was Clifford Cardinal.

My second presentation was in the evening where I was due to co-present a paper with my dear friend John Hunter. John had created a beautiful painting illustrating an important historical story about a long ago time when humanity faced environmental crisis and how healers had interceded to assist. Shortly before the conference John had to pull out of the trip because of needing to care for his mother due to health and family challenges.

So I stayed in touch with John and he gave me instructions on how to present his part of the presentation. I spent the first half of my talk speaking about John and my appreciation of him. Then I spoke about the story behind the painting and finally how this ancient story of environmental crisis and redemption had parallels in modern times for appreciating the role of healers in assisting humanity to emerge through this time.

John had advised me that this painting was to be offered as a gift to someone associated with the conference organisers and left it to me to decide. At lunch the next day I saw Clifford sitting with some other Elders. Again I felt there was something very special about this man. I went over to one of the organisers, another dear friend who had actually initially invited me to the conference, Meda DeWitt Schleifman. Meda is a Tlingit traditional healer from Alaska. I mentioned to her my sense of admiration for the spiritual radiance of this man even though I did not know anything about him and that I felt that the painting I had been given was meant to go to him. She said she thought this was a good idea as well. She explained that he was on the organising committee of the conference, he was a powerful Cree healer and also a Professor of Medicine in the University Hospital. One of the reasons for the presence of so many senior healers from around North America at this gathering was due to the respect they have for Clifford.

I went over to Clifford's table and let him know I wanted to give him something, however it needed to be done in a sacred way and I wasn't sure what the right time for that would be. An Elder next to Clifford spoke up first, "there is a sweat lodge ceremony some of us are going to later today. You are welcome to come."

So later that afternoon I made it to the ceremony. Before it started I went up to a truck where Clifford was sitting talking with a Navajo Elder. I waited until he motioned me over and let him know I had the gift for him. He got out of his truck and started walking with me towards a building where some of the people were gathered. I carried the painting over and he motioned for the Navajo Elder to come join us. When we went inside Clifford and the other Elder sat down in the corner and I began to share with Clifford the background to it and who John was. Clifford asked if I want to share this with everyone and then softly spoke something in Cree. Suddenly everyone who had been talking with each other stopped and turned their attention toward us. I felt I must now sing a prayer to begin and so I sang and then I unrolled the painting. Clifford and the other Navajo Elder each took one end of the painting to hold it for all to see. I again expressed my respect for John Hunter and what he had painted and then shared the story of the painting, told as best I could. When I finished I remembered John's instructions to me to roll the painting a certain way to preserve it from cracking. I began to reach for the painting and saw that both Elders began to roll it up themselves. I had a brief moment of panic where my ego was wanting to say "Wait, there's a special way to roll the painting." I then saw they rolled it up exactly the way John had taught me. Later I felt really humbled and embarrassed about my private thoughts when I found out that both of these Elders are master artists. Once they had rolled it up and it was given to Clifford he said, "I will respond to this gift at the conference dinner."

At the conference dinner I remember hoping to be able to sit next to Clifford. I walked in and saw that he was sitting with a group of Elders and it didn't look like I would have that privilege. I sat at a table with the senior Navajo Elder and I invited the guest next to me to sit near him so they could meet and talk. Later a woman with a beautiful turquoise necklace came in and asked to sit next to him saying that he is a cultural father for her. I was quiet most of the time. Although I did ask her at one point what she does. She said, "I'm between jobs at the moment." A few minutes later the welcoming speeches began and then they introduced the keynote speaker, a surgeon of great renown, someone that had recently been shortlisted to become the next Surgeon General of the United States. They said her name and the woman next to me, the noble Navajo woman who was "between jobs" stood up, walked to the front and began her keynote speech. I think I had a pretty big smile throughout her entire talk.

When the talk finished there were some beautiful cultural performances and then Clifford stood up and announced that they were having a blanket give away for the Elders. One by one they called Elders from around the room to give them each a blanket. After that was complete I settled into my seat to wait for whatever was to come next. Clifford then started talking about someone and that they had come from across the world, far to the south and that they had brought honour with a special gift. He then held a blanket and called my name to the front. I was truly surprised. I had thought he was going to speak to me privately or at another time in the evening. I walked up feeling incredibly humbled and in awe. One of the drummers asked if they should play the same song as was being played for previous blanket give-aways and Clifford said, "Play the honour song." I felt amazed and blessed beyond anything I could expect.

The following day was the last day of the conference. I still hadn't had more than a few sentences of conversation with Clifford and yet I still felt this call from my ancestors to "be obedient" even though I had no idea what that meant. As people were packing things up I asked the conference photographer if she would take a picture of Clifford and me together to send to me later.

After the photo was taken I told Clifford about my feeling that my ancestors were asking me to be obedient in assisting him in some way but that I didn't know what that was. He said, "Move back to Edmonton. I am starting a clinic of traditional medicine. You can work with me." I did not expect to hear him say that at all. I don't remember exactly what I said in response, however it was something like, "That will be good."

When I returned home to Melbourne, Australia, I told Lisa about meeting an amazing Medicine Man, although I didn't tell her his name. I shared my impressions of his radiating great humility and sacrifice for humanity. Some days later the photographer, Riva Benditt, sent me the photo of Clifford and me. I brought my laptop over to Lisa and said, "See, here he is."

Lisa looked and her mouth dropped open.

"That's Clifford! I know him! He had long braids when I knew him and he held his head tilted like that!" I was totally stunned. "What? You know him?" Lisa said, "Yes, he was at my school at Saddle Lake Cree Nation. Onchaminahos school. I was only six, but I remember that I liked him being around. He felt steady, humble. Send the photo to Tish, and maybe she might remember the specifics better." I sent the photo to Lisa's older sister, Tish to see if she remembered. Shortly after, she replied "Of course! He was Lisa's grade 2 or 3 teacher [In addition to Mrs Henry and Miss Kimball, respectively.] Also he is a member of the family who defined my experience on Saddle Lake. They were family, mentors, ambassadors and changed forever the way I would see and move through the world. Big Love & respect."

Immediately I wrote to Clifford to let him know of my discovery that he was one of Lisa's educators when she was a child. His email response completely blew me away. He explained that Lisa's father, Ron Silvers had been his principal and had done a "very, very good" job of mentoring him. Clifford wrote that he had gone on to carry those pillars in education throughout his career. He wrote, "I have photos of Tish and her sister in dancing regalia, something we started when Ron was Principal. In that picture are most of the members of the well-known Pow Wow group Northern Cree, they were just starting up. Yea Ron Silvers had something to do with the Cree coming back and developing the pride of their tribal group."

In a time when Cree language and culture were forbidden in schools, Lisa's father, Ron Silvers had been among the first to encourage the teaching of Cree culture, language, song and dance. As I read out Clifford's words my wife began to cry, not having realised her father's contribution to humanity in this way. It was just how things were when she was a child. She didn't know that what had happened in her school was an historical first.

The other part of Clifford's email that filled me with wonder was this: Clifford explained that in the 1990s he used traditional knowledge to develop an HIV medicine for people in the community. A researcher had then taken that knowledge and developed it into a pharmaceutical medicine called Indinivar. Upon looking this medicine up I found that the World Health Organisation had listed this HIV medicine Clifford developed as one of the world's "essential medicines".

I was stunned. Now I understood part of why he came up to me to say my presentation honouring Indigenous contributions to HIV medicines was meaningful to him. I still didn't understand why my ancestors had asked me to be obedient to Clifford, but something miraculous was emerging.

I had to get back to Edmonton. I felt very, very urgent about this. But how? I was doing mostly pro-bono work for Indigenous communities and I had no income. The university had paid for my flight the first time. How could I afford to go back to Canada to spend time with Clifford? I wrote to Clifford and said I would pray and ask my ancestors for assistance to get back to him.

Now going back a step to March 2015, on my way back to Melbourne from that first visit to Canada, I met my daughter May in Sydney. I shared with her some of the stories of what happened when I was on that trip. She turned to me and said, "Dad, when are you going to write a book about your life? If you don't, I will." I've had many people ask me to write, but it wasn't until the moment when my own child asked me to write that a flood of words suddenly emerged. (One of my editors reminded me of May's purity and her clarity of vision in knowing what needed to happen.) One of the chapters in *Nudges from Grandfather*, Wisdom Man in Action, was written at the request of another author, Camilla Chance, for use in her book, *Wisdom Man in Action*. I decided it would fit nicely in the book that May had asked me to write and so I called Camilla to ask her permission to duplicate the chapter in *Nudges*.

When I called Camilla I asked her how she was going with *Wisdom Man in Action*, a book about how the life of Aboriginal Elder, Banjo Clarke, had affected the lives of others. Some of the stories showed that people's lives had been affected just by reading his biography Wisdom Man, also written by Camilla and a best-seller with Penguin. Camilla explained to me that the project was on hold as the previous editor hadn't quite worked out. I found myself asking her, "What do you need?" and she asked if I would help her edit the book. I said, "Well I don't have any professional editing background, but I can perhaps form a team of people with those skills and who can assist. Send me the chapters that you have and I will read through them and begin that process." Camilla responded that chapters hadn't been written yet. I asked how could I edit the book if the chapters hadn't been written yet. She explained that there was quite a bit of correspondence, but also that I would need to travel to meet people whose lives had been affected by Banjo and interview them and then write down the results. I asked her, "So what's the first chapter?" She explained that there was a Native American group in California that had a ceremony in 2009 on Palm Sunday and that Banjo had visited them in spirit and asked them to come to Uluru to perform a healing ceremony for the people and land in Australia. One year later they flew to Uluru and performed their ceremony on Palm Sunday again. I paused and said, "When is Palm Sunday again?" She said, "The first Sunday after Easter." Again I paused and leaned over to look at the calendar. I expressed with amazement, "Today is Palm Sunday!". She said, I'll fly you to California and you can interview them and other Indigenous people whose lives have been affected by Banjo." I asked her, "Where will I go after California?" She said, "I want you to travel with Banjo's grandson, John Clarke. He's been invited to a Native American water blessing ceremony for Battle River. Someone read a passage out of *Wisdom Man* at an earlier year's ceremony and the Native people present resonated with Banjo's words about the forest and the 'little people' and Banjo's family has been invited there. I want you to attend with John and to document what happens there for one of the chapters." I asked her, "Where is the Battle River water blessing ceremony happening?" She replied: "A town called Camrose."

I Googled the map location of Camrose where Camilla was sending me and found that it's a one hour drive from Clifford's home. One week after writing to Clifford to assure him that I would pray to my ancestors to find a way to get back to him, I knew I was going. I was completely unprepared for what happened next.

To contact the author, download the audio book, discover additional resources or to pre-order the book

Medicine of Our Ancestors

go to

www.chriskavelin.com

www.ingramcontent.com/pod-product-compliance
Lightning Source LLC
Chambersburg PA
CBHW021403290426
44108CB00010B/361